TEAM DEVELOPMENT MANUAL

For James and Victoria

Team
Development Manual

MIKE WOODCOCK

Gower

First published by
Gower Press, Teakfield Limited
Reprinted 1982, 1983, 1984 by Gower Publishing Company Limited,
Croft Road, Aldershot, Hants, GU11 3HR, England

British Library Cataloguing in Publication Data

Woodcock, Mike
   Team development manual.
   1. Work groups 2. Management
   I. Title
   658.4'02   HD51

ISBN 0 566 02115 3 ✓

Printed and bound in Great Britain by
Biddles Ltd, Guildford and King's Lynn

Contents

Preface

Organisations are about people working together and, therefore, developing effective teams must be a prime responsibility of all who manage or lead groups of people. Although library shelves abound with volumes about the theory of management, little is available in the way of practical help to those who have the responsibility of leading and developing people in teams. This manual is an attempt to provide that help. Firstly, it gives guidance about how teams can be made more effective and, secondly, it presents a range of resources which can be used in a practical way to bring this about. The resources include many well-tried activities and techniques as well as a series of lecturettes which explain the essentials of team development. Finally, it gives some leads on where to obtain further ideas and help.

Throughout, my aim has been to keep each section as short and simple as possible because this manual is written primarily for busy people who want practical help rather than elaborate theory. I have used all of the material presented in organisational teambuilding assignments, in workshops, on seminars and in other teambuilding sessions or in my own businesses. The teambuilding events on which the material has been used range from directors' meetings to evening seminars, from in-company formal training events to residential workshops and from one-to-one coaching sessions to national conferences involving hundreds of people. Margarine manufacturers, electronics engineers, builders, bakers, mechanical engineers, accountants, consultants, brewers, company directors, wholesalers, retailers, magistrates, secretaries, training officers, milk processors, general managers, supervisors, clerks and many more have joined in the activities and helped to improve many of them.

I hope the manual will have a variety of uses. It can simply be read to give a grasp of teamwork concepts or it can be utilised as a source of ideas for anyone wishing to undertake practical teambuilding activities, or it can be used as a complete approach to organisational teambuilding programmes. To the manager it should be a source of practical ideas to implement in his own organisation, to the student a source of theory and experiment and to the skilled facilitator a source of further ideas and developmental activities.

THE LAYOUT

The decision to call this work a manual was of great importance as its success will not be determined by the number of copies sold, nor by the number who read it. It will be successful if it leads people to take action, to translate theory into practice in their own organisations, businesses, clubs or groups. Because of that I have laid out the material in a way which will enable it to be readily available for practical use.

Part I is about how to improve team performance. In eight separate sections it clarifies understanding of the principal characteristics of effective work teams, provides a unique instrument which helps to establish the development needs of such teams, gives guidance on action planning, presents a set of groundrules for team development, outlines the limits of teambuilding, suggests ways of designing team-building events, and gives a guide to Part II.

Part II is a collection of resources which can be used to improve team performance. The first section provides a collection of team-building activities which can be used both in practical work situations and on teambuilding events. Although the ideas are laid out as individual 'activities' which the facilitator can use as such, he can also link them to form longer training sessions or modify them to suit his own particular needs. The second section is a collection of lecturettes derived from established teambuilding theory. They can be used as inputs on training courses and teambuilding events or can be read to give a basic understanding of teamwork concepts. All the items in these two sections have been used successfully by me on team-building assignments.

Part III is a source of further ideas. It tells the user where to go for further help and advice about teambuilding and will be particularly useful to those who wish to study and practise teambuilding at a deeper level than that for which this manual provides.

THE LANGUAGE

It is said that a psychologist is someone who tells you something you already know in a language which you cannot understand. Inevitably in any trade or profession words are used which convey a great deal to those who regularly use them but are seen as 'jargon' or 'unnecessarily technical' by those who do not. This book aims to bridge the gap between the professional who works in the team development area and the manager, team leader and team member by presenting theory and practice in a down-to-earth way.

Frequently managers do not read books about management because they find them dull, uninteresting and full of jargon. They also find that often they are strong on theory but weak on practice. Therefore, I established three groundrules to guide me in writing this book. They were:

1   That its language should be down-to-earth, free from jargon and readily understood by those who will use it.
2   That it should strive to simplify theory.
3   That the emphasis should be on practical things which the reader can do for himself within his own team and which he will find enjoyable, stimulating and useful.

I hope that you find these aims have been met.

MIKE WOODCOCK
January 1979

Acknowledgements

The ideas in this manual come from so many sources that it would be impossible to acknowledge them all even if I knew them, which I do not. However, where sources have been identified they have been acknowledged in the text, and books which I have found particularly valuable have been listed in Part III.

There are four special acknowledgements I wish to give. Firstly, to colleagues at the Food, Drink and Tobacco Industry Training Board who have shared with me the running of many teambuilding workshops – particularly Tony Booth, Chris Creswick, Rennie Fritchie, Sue Kerrison and Roy Williams. They have all contributed greatly to whatever knowledge I have on this subject and they are all very stimulating people to work with. Secondly, to Dave Francis, my partner, friend and co-author of my first book *People at Work: A Practical Guide to Organisational Change*, for the many ideas which we have developed together. Thirdly, to Jill Evans who not only typed the drafts but so readily gave me the feedback I needed when I was not following my own groundrules.

Finally I thank all those who have mapped out this field before me. The many writers, consultants and teachers who have continually developed ways of helping teams become more effective and on whose experience I have drawn in my work and in the preparation of this book.

PART I

IMPROVING TEAMWORK

Part I contains eight sections.

1 *What is teamwork?* Some of the symptoms of poor teamwork are described and the characteristics of effective teamwork are outlined.

2 *The stages of team development* The four essential stages are described to help teams to understand team development.

3 *The limitations of teambuilding* This is included to show that teambuilding solutions may be applied inappropriately.

4 *Diagnosing teamwork problems* This section contains a unique instrument which serves both to develop understanding of the theory of teambuilding and to begin assessing the strengths and weaknesses of your own team. It can be used to decide which of the 'building blocks of effective teamwork' you will use to improve the performance of your own team.

5 *Action planning* A simple form of planning to help you take teambuilding decisions in a logical and sensible order.

6 *Groundrules for team development* Some basic 'dos and don'ts' about teambuilding presented as a checklist which you can use to guide all of your teambuilding efforts.

7 *Designing teambuilding events* To help you in planning tailor-made teambuilding events, some guidelines for designing events are included together with examples of how the theory and activities in this book can be used to form the basis of learning events.

8 *Selecting teambuilding activities* This provides a unique link between the 'building blocks of effective teamwork' and the teambuilding activities in Part II. It will help you choose appropriate activities for your team.

By using these eight sections you will avoid one of the major problems of development – the potential gap between theory and practice.

1
What is teamwork?

Organisations are essentially about people working together and yet so often they fail to capitalise upon the full potential of this. A team can accomplish much more than the sum of its individual members and yet frequently groups of people are seen to achieve less than could have been accomplished by the individual members working alone. Most organisations have meetings which dampen inspiration and departments which seem to devote more energy to maintaining their own organisational position than to the common good of the organisation as a whole. Teamwork is individuals working together to accomplish more than they could alone, but, more than that, it can be exciting, satisfying and enjoyable. Perhaps the simplest analogy is with that of the football team. Were any of us to be given the task of building up a new national team we know that the task would involve much more than just obtaining the eleven best players in the nation. The success of the team would depend not only upon individual skills but on the way those individuals supported and worked with each other. The good football team is much more than a collection of individual skills; it is these skills used in a way which produces a united effort. Similarly, with almost any kind of team, its success, its very existence, depends upon the way in which all play together.

Over the past few years we have seen many approaches aimed at increasing organisational effectiveness and organisations today pay more and more attention to the training and development of their people, particularly those who hold managerial positions. Most of that development activity is centred upon the improvement of individual skills, knowledge and experience, but organisations are

increasingly finding that this is not enough, that a real key to success
is the way in which individuals behave towards each other and the
way in which groups of people relate to and work with each other.
Teamwork improves these things.

How then do we recognise where good teamwork and bad teamwork flourish? Perhaps, as with most things, it is easier to start with
the bad than the good, so let us look at some of the symptoms of
bad teamwork.

First there is the symptom of frustration. As organisations get
larger the opportunities for personal expression and satisfaction often
become less. Too frequently people who work in organisations become frustrated because they can no longer see a clear way of meeting
their own needs and aspirations. People just lose inspiration and lack
the commitment and motivation which are essential ingredients of
effective teamwork.

In many organisations the symptoms of grumbling and retaliation
are easily seen. Because people cannot express themselves through
the system they do it privately in discussions in the corridors, lava-
tories and car parks. Often bar room chat is a better indicator of
organisational health than the most elaborate attitude surveys. The
organisations that experience poor teamwork also seem to spend a lot
of time on retaliations. They do not use mistakes as opportunities
for increased learning and improvement but as excuses for punishing
those who made the mistakes, and they do this in the many and
varied ways in which organisations are able to hand out punishments.

Unhealthy competition is another indicator of poor teamwork.
Competition is the life-blood of many organisations but there is
a great difference between the kind of healthy competition where
people can enjoy the just rewards of their deserved success and others
can accept that the best man, system or policy succeeded, and the
kind of organisation where backbiting, 'dirty tricks' and politics are
the everyday pastimes of managers. Similarly great differences in
rivalry between departments may be found. Many organisations owe
much of their success to the natural competitive spirit which exists
between departments and to the pride of team membership which
departmentalisation often brings, but many others have departments
which are at constant war with each other, each jockeying for
superior organisational position, influence or perks. One particular
organisation was characterised for many years by the constant
bickering and 'dirty tricks' of its heads of departments, each depart-
mental head taking advantage over the others whenever possible. Not

only did that lead to the organisation as a whole missing opportunities, but many more junior employees found that although they wanted to work with others organisational barriers had been erected between them and their counterparts in other departments.

Another sound indicator of poor teamwork is simply the expression which employees wear on their faces. Effective teamwork breeds happiness and the uninformed visitor can often get an immediate impression of whether work is a happy place to be or whether he is likely to be 'killed in the rush' if he is around at 'clocking off' time. Work does not have to be a dull and unenjoyable place; it can so easily be a really rewarding place where people love to be.

To many who have studied organisations, openness and honesty are the key indicators of organisational health. Unfortunately, some people seem to try honesty only when everything else has failed. Many managers particularly seem to go to enormous lengths to avoid telling the truth. There are, of course, occasions in every organisation where something other than total openness is necessary but where good teamwork exists there is generally no need for locks on drawers, dishonest statements to employees and the taking of false bargaining stances.

Meetings are another key indicator of teamwork. The main reason for having meetings is to utilise the collective skills of a group of people whilst working on common problems or opportunities. Too often, however, we experience meetings which in no way use these skills, meetings where only one or a few people contribute, and meetings where many managers seem to use the occasion as an opportunity to lay down the rules rather than utilise the resources of the team. The quality of meetings can usually be determined by the way in which individuals either look forward to or dread the normal weekly or monthly get together.

In many organisations the quality of relationship between managers and those they manage is so low that effective teamwork just cannot get off the ground. Where people cannot confide in or trust their manager, where they are fearful of him or where their conversations are on a superficial or trivial level then real teamwork is unlikely to exist. Essentially teamwork engenders high quality relationships. Another sign of low quality relationships is often that the leader becomes increasingly isolated from his team. He does not represent their view and they do not subscribe to his. The effective team leader needs to be very much a part of his team.

People just not developing is another sure sign of ineffective teamwork. If a team is to be effective it needs to be continually developing itself and this in part means constantly facilitating individual as well as team development. Often development does not happen because:

(a) there are perceived or real time pressures;
(b) it is seen as the job of the personnel department or training officer;
(c) conflict exists between the team's culture and that of the organisation;
(d) team leaders lack the skills or willingness to make it happen;
(e) there is fear of the consequences of development.

Sometimes poor teamwork results in jobs getting done twice or not at all because no clear understanding of roles within and between teams exists. Sometimes although common problems exist people are just not able or willing to get together and work on them.

Then there is the attitude which teams and individual members have to the possibility of external help. The ineffective team will usually either reject offers of help because it fears the consequences of outsiders finding out what the team is really like or will seize all offers of help because it lacks any coherent view of how to proceed and is content to hand over its problems to someone else. The effective team will use external help constructively by recognising the unique contribution and viewpoint which it can bring, but it will always maintain ownership of its own problems and its own destiny.

Creativity is a delicate flower which only flourishes in the right conditions, mainly conditions of personal freedom and support; freedom to experiment, try out ideas and concepts and support from those who listen, evaluate and offer help. A dearth of new ideas generally goes with poor teamwork because it is within teams that the conditions for creativity can most easily be created.

The degree to which people help and use each other is another indicator. Where effective teamwork does not exist people tend to work in isolation and neither offer nor receive the help of their colleagues. All of us need that help in order to perform at our optimum level.

The conditions described above are indicative of an unhealthy organisation and all of them can be significantly improved by effective teamwork.

What then are the characteristics of effective teamwork? Very simply they are the opposites of what is described above.

People can and do express themselves honestly and openly. Conversation about work is the same both inside and outside the organisation. Mistakes are faced openly and used as vehicles for learning and difficult situations are confronted.

Helpful competition and conflict of ideas are used constructively and team members have a pride in the success of their team. Unhelpful competition and conflict have been eliminated.

Good relationships exist with other teams and departments. Each values and respects the other and their respective leaders themselves comprise an effective team.

Personal relationships are characterised by support and trust, with people helping each other whenever possible.

Meetings are productive and stimulating with all participating and feeling ownership of the actions which result from the decisions made. New ideas abound and their use enables the team to stay ahead.

Boss-subordinate relationships are sound, each helping the other to perform his role better, and the team feels that it is led in an appropriate way.

Personal and individual development is highly rated and opportunities are constantly sought for making development happen.

There is clear agreement about and understanding of objectives and of the roles which the team and its individual members will play in achieving them.

External help will be welcomed and used where appropriate.

Finally, the team regularly reviews where it is going, why it needs to go there, and how it is getting there. If necessary, it alters its practices in the light of that review.

All of this means that "work" is a happy place to be; people enjoy themselves wherever possible but this enjoyment is conducive to achievement, not a barrier to it. People get satisfaction from their working lives and work is one of the places where they meet their needs and aspirations.

These characteristics can be seen as the raw materials of effective teamwork. I like to see them as 'building blocks' because they are what we can use in a very practical way to build effective teams. Stated as simply as possible they are –

| Clear objectives and agreed goals |
| Openness and confrontation |
| Support and trust |
| Co-operation and conflict |
| Sound procedures |
| Appropriate leadership |
| Regular review |
| Individual development |
| Sound inter-group relations |

In Part II of this manual there is a separate 'lecturette' about each of these building blocks.

2
The stages of team development

As teams become increasingly effective so the characteristics they display and the procedures they adopt also change. Even where teams have not tried consciously to improve their methods of operation and effectiveness there can be tremendous differences, but where serious efforts are made to improve these things observers have noted that there are common characteristics which tend to be exhibited according to the stage of development. Before exhibiting the signs of effective teamwork which were listed in '1 What is teamwork?' often a team will need to pass through several stages of development during which other signs or characteristics will be exhibited.

Any attempt at defining these stages and the characteristics associated with them must be an over-simplification. However, a simple model based on four essential stages of development is very useful in helping teams to understand team development and also to understand and agree where they are in the development process. It must be remembered, however, that no team ever exhibits solely the characteristics of one particular stage, rather it is a question of which characteristics are the most prominent. A grouping, even though crude, does help a team to understand something of where it is in the development process and of where it wants to be, and many have found this simple four-stage model useful (see page 14).

STAGE 1: THE UNDEVELOPED TEAM

This is the most common stage of development to be found in organisations. It abounds wherever people have come together to complete a task but have devoted little or no time to considering how they should or do operate.

One characteristic of this stage is that feelings are not dealt with, usually because it is not seen as appropriate to consider the way others feel and certainly not to discuss feelings openly. Generally, emotions are seen as something only appropriate to one's private life with the workplace being for work. If feelings and emotions do come to the fore they are usually immediately brushed under the carpet. People conform to the established line, often because that is the way in which things have always been done and sometimes because they are too scared to suggest changes. Even constructive ideas about change are not welcomed and people usually learn that it is safer not to 'rock the boat' by making unwanted suggestions. This usually results in people being disheartened and leadership seldom being challenged. Little care is shown for other people or their views and this is frequently characterised by a lot of talking and little real listening. Meetings tend to mainly comprise a series of statements with pople queueing to put their point of view without listening to what goes before or after. Personal weaknesses are covered up because the group lacks the skill to support or to eliminate them. Mistakes are used as 'evidence' to help convict people rather than as opportunities to learn. There is no shared understanding of what needs to be done and often the leader has a different view to those he is trying to lead. Where there is clarity this is often because people's instructions have come from the top rather than because they have shared in the deter-mination of plans. Mistakes are frequently covered up by individuals as they know that they will be seen as failure and this means that team members do not get the opportunity to learn from their mis-takes and improve. Outside threats are met by defensiveness, increased bureaucracy, paperwork and rules. People confine themselves to their own defined jobs and the boss takes most of the decisions.

It needs to be said that many apparently effective teams show these characteristics, but this is usual only if the boss has the wisdom, energy and time to make all the decisions. This is not real teamwork as it does not capitalise on the dormant strengths of the team. Some-times this stage is referred to as the 'king and court' stage because the team resembles the old concept of the 'court' who would never dare to seriously challenge the judgement of their 'king'.

The greatest single leap forward in team development is when a team leaves stage 1 and enters stage 2 because that is when it takes a decision to do something serious about improving things.

STAGE 2: THE EXPERIMENTING TEAM

Stage 2 can begin when the team decides that it wants to seriously review its operating methods and undertake activities which will improve its performance. It is this willingness which is the distinguishing characteristic of the stage 2 team. The team begins to be willing to experiment; to sail in what, for them, are uncharted waters, and face the ensuing opportunities and dangers. Other features of this stage of development are that problems are faced more openly and wider options are considered before decisions are taken. Where necessary the underlying values and beliefs affecting decisions begin to be debated and this often leads to temporary feelings of insecurity and high risks. As more risky issues are opened up hitherto taboo topics begin to be discussed and often the way in which the team is managed is one of the first issues examined. More personal issues are raised, feelings begin to be considered and personal animosities begin to be dealt with. People begin to say things which they may have wanted to mention for years. This can obviously lead to some traumatic encounters between team members but they quickly learn that when the dirt has been put on the table and examined the team becomes a healthier and happier place to be.

The group inevitably becomes more inward looking, and for a time may even reject other groups and individuals. This is a transient phase and is because the team has become so interested and obsessed with its own problems and new horizons that it just wants to work on them and sees that as the most important thing to do. More concern is shown for the views and problems of colleagues with a consequent increase in real listening, and, often for the first time, people begin to understand other members of the team. Meetings begin to be characterised by more listening and thinking and less talking. In this stage teams can often become uncomfortable but they are also dynamic and exciting. The observer can see things coming to life and people who have been dormant for years start to really contribute. However, although the team has become more open and potentially more effective it still lacks the capacity to act in an economic, unified and methodical way.

It has worked on some of the interpersonal issues successfully but it has not yet put this learning to profitable use.

STAGE 3: THE CONSOLIDATING TEAM

After the team has worked on the interpersonal issues of stage 2 and has begun to resolve them it will begin to have the confidence, open approach and trust to examine its operating methods. Generally the team decides to adopt a more systematic approach which leads to a clearer and more methodical way of working. The rules and procedures which characterised stage 1 now begin to be re-introduced but this time they are not edicts from on high or historical precedents which have to be observed, they are the agreed operating rules of the team, which everyone has had a part in framing and to which everyone is committed. Even with the better relationships built in stage 2, the team quickly learns that groundrules are still important. The most apparent evidence of this is the way in which decisions are taken, usually by:

- (a)   clarifying the purpose of the task or activity;
- (b)   establishing the objectives which need to be met;
- (c)   collecting the information which will be needed;
- (d)   considering the options which are open to the team;
- (e)   detailed planning of what needs to be done;
- (f)   reviewing the outcome and using it as a basis for improving future operations.

The improved relationships and more exciting methods experienced in stage 2 are maintained but they are used to build the groundrules and working procedures which the team will use.

STAGE 4: THE MATURE TEAM

After stage 3 has been worked through there is the basis for a really mature team. The openness, concern and improved relationships of stage 2 and the systematic approach of stage 3 can now be used to complete the task of building a really mature team.

Flexibility becomes the keynote, with different procedures being adopted to meet different needs. People are not concerned with defending positions. Leadership is decided by the situation not protocol, the group itself recognising the kind of leadership which is necessary and the leader recognising the need to involve the team in matters of substance. Often formal management hierarchy is abandoned in favour of something which the team feels is more appropriate. Everyone's energies are utilised for the team, because individual commitment to team success exists. There is pride in the team and its achievements but this does not stifle individual initiative and achievement because everyone realises that people are happier and more effective when they are able to meet their needs and aspirations. The team considers essential principles and social aspects of its decisions. It realises not only that it is part of a larger organisation but also that organisations have a moral and social responsibility. It begins to realise that it is part of a big world and can help others as well. Development becomes an increasing priority because all realise that continued success depends on continued development. Trust, openness, honesty, co-operation and confrontation, and a continual review of results become part of the way of life. The desire to improve further means that external help is always welcome. The team is not only admired but is emulated and it is always willing to reach out and help other less mature teams. Above all the team is a happy and rewarding place to be.

Stage 4	Experimentation. Risky issues debated. Wider options considered. Personal feelings raised. More listening. Concern for others.	plus	Methodical working. Agreed procedures. Established groundrules.	plus	High flexibility. Appropriate leadership. Maximum use of energy and ability. Essential principles and social aspects considered. Needs of all met. Development a priority.	
Stage 3	Experimentation. Risky issues debated. Wider options considered. Personal feelings raised. More listening. Concern for others.	plus	Methodical working. Agreed procedures. Established groundrules.			
Stage 2	Experimentation. Risky issues debated. Wider options considered. Personal feelings raised. More listening. Concern for others.					
Stage 1	Feelings not dealt with. Workplace is for work. Established line prevails. Not 'rocking the boat'. Poor listening. Weaknesses covered up. Unclear objectives. Low involvement in planning. Bureaucracy. Boss takes most decisions.					

Summary of the four stages of team development

3
The limitations of teambuilding

Reading only a few current management magazines is sufficient to indicate which of the various techniques or theories for improving the effectiveness of individuals or organisations are in fashion. It is perhaps inevitable that writers, advisers and people whose profession is helping organisations themselves become relatively easily interested in new or exciting theories and techniques. Unfortunately, the victims of their enthusiasm are often those whom they seek to help. Many advisers and consultants are known to tour the country with a solution in their briefcase looking for a problem to fit it, and often they find such a problem whether or not it really exists. Similarly, in some organisations there are training officers who are tempted to see problems which are not there simply to try out a new technique which particularly appeals to them.

Teamwork is increasingly being seen as an important subject and teambuilding is now one of the most popular and effective ways of improving the health of an organisation. There is then a very acute danger that teambuilding solutions may be applied inappropriately, that well-meaning but misdirected people may go through the 'ritual dances' of teambuilding when the problems of the organisation are really quite different.

Over the past few years I have led a great many 'teamwork workshops', events at which managers, directors and training officers have been introduced to the theory of teambuilding. All have been characterised by the enthusiasm which is generated and the desire of participants to engage in teambuilding activities not only at the event but also when they returned to their organisations. Because of this I have always insisted on including a session which aims to put teamwork problems into the context of the whole range of 'people problems' which an organisation may face. It is so easy to rush into teambuilding activities when teamwork is not the problem.

There are many definitions and models of the 'people problems' which organisations can face but the one which I generally use was developed by Dave Francis and myself and is explained in greater detail in *People at Work: A Practical Guide to Organisational Change* [1]. The aim of this chapter is not to delve into other problems but merely to show that there are many issues to do with people which organisations commonly face and which will not be solved solely by improved teamwork. It is true that, to a certain extent, all 'people problems' are interrelated and any solutions will overlap but it is also important that before taking action there is agreement that teamwork is central to the problem. Although improved teamwork will help people to confront and solve almost any problem the following ten groups of 'people problems' will not be solved solely by the kind of approaches contained in this book, because they are not essentially teamwork problems.

POOR RECRUITMENT AND SELECTION

Whenever a business operates people have to be hired and, although most organisations have vast experience of this area, so often the root of an organisation's 'people problems' lies simply in the wrong people being selected. Either they have the wrong skills or the wrong personality. Sometimes those who carry out the selection lack the required skills, sometimes they are the wrong people to be making the selection, and sometimes the organisation is unclear about the kind of people it really requires. Often, in spite of elaborate personnel departments, policies and procedures are unclear. No amount of teambuilding will make square pegs fit round roles!

CONFUSED ORGANISATION STRUCTURE

Everything bigger than a one man unit needs some organisation. It can take many forms but most businesses tend to be based on a hierarchical system. Usually the boss sits at the top and beneath him other levels of management span out like a pyramid. Usually lines of responsibility and authority are clearly and explicitly stated. Hierarchical organisations are usually fine where repetitive tasks need to be accomplished and deadlines need to be met but it can be disastrous where creativity and initiative are required and where innovation is the keynote of success. Here a more flexible, free-ranging organisational form is often required which will enable people to experiment, to step out of line and fly their own kites. If the way people are organised is alien to the task being performed, again teambuilding will do little more than expose the problem; it will not in itself solve it.

One particular organisation continually faced a dilemma in the way in which it was organised. Fundamentally, this organisation needed to have lots of new ideas, to develop them and to experiment and then to apply them. Although the greater part of the organisation was, and always would be, engaged in applying the developed ideas, it needed as its very lifeblood the creative people who could conceive new approaches and experiment with and develop them. Here was the classic example of a group of highly creative people who required freedom to experiment, living alongside a group of people who needed to produce results and meet deadlines. For years the whole organisation constantly moved between an organisational form which was conducive to the work of the first group and one which suited the second. When creativity was suited complaints of sloppiness, passed deadlines and low output came to the fore. This resulted in a tighter, more controllable structure which in turn stifled the creative people and led to fewer ideas, less experimentation and less development. Managers regularly nailed their colours to one mast or the other and careers were made and lost with increasing rapidity as the pendulum kept swinging. Eventually the organisation came to its senses and recognised that both approaches were right and that it had to live with two different organisational forms. The ideas and development people opted for a 'matrix' organisation, in this case one in which each person had two lines of responsibility, one to his line manager and one to a development leader. The others opted for a more conventional 'hierarchical' organisational form. One basis for effective teamwork was thus formed.

Another symptom of poor organisation is the 'over-developed limb'. Sometimes a particular department, function or individual becomes so powerful that their part of the organisation becomes far too large or influential for the good of the whole. It is like a body with an arm which is twice as long as it should be – the whole is handicapped by the part. Problems like this need to be dealt with before effective teamwork across an organisation can begin.

LACK OF CONTROL

This is often very similar to, and related to, poor organisation because it is through organisation that control is usually exercised. The way in which people are 'controlled' can be either a very positive or a very negative force. Over-control can lead to initiative being stifled and potentially valuable contributions being lost. Most people are quite capable of controlling their own contributions and actions within a reasonably loose framework of overall accountability and, naturally, they resent unnecessary external controls. However, most people also recognise the necessity for sensible control and do not resent control which is in the right hands and which is understood and agreed. They realise that an organisation which is out of control is like a ship in a storm without a rudder, i.e., it is at the mercy of the weather and likely to be wrecked on the rocks. Teambuilding in an atmosphere of over-control will not work because people will lack the basic freedom to either agree principles or put them into practice. Similarly, it will not work in an atmosphere of anarchy where no basic disciplines are accepted or used.

POOR TRAINING

Keeping up with present-day changes is an ever-increasing problem for today's managers, often requiring more and more learning to be undertaken in little available time. One of the hallmarks of an effective team is that the skills and knowledge of its participants are continually reviewed, updated and improved, but everyone needs certain skills and some knowledge to even begin playing their part in a team. In most organisations there are induction courses and facilities for initial training, coupled with facilities for ensuring that people are able to attend external events and so obtain the skills and knowledge which the organisation cannot impart. Effective teambuilding can help identify both deficiencies and opportunities for increased learning and also help personal development, but it will not take the place of the fundamental learning opportunities which every organisation needs to give to its employees. Crucial to teambuilding is the learning climate and the overall receptivity to learning. Before almost any development activity can take place people need to welcome new learning and not feel threatened by it. Before team development can take place, training policy methods and practice need to be resolved.

LOW MOTIVATION

The way people feel about the organisation they work in has a great deal to do with the amount of effort they are prepared to put into their working lives. Employees' views about the organisation they work for are often formed even before they enter through the door. For example, the organisation may have a reputation in the local or the national community, and it will have its own recruitment practices. The moment a new employee walks through the door he really starts to form, alter or confirm his opinion, based on the experiences he undergoes. An immediate impression may be gained of the level of motivation in many organisations. In some places you could be 'killed in the rush' as people depart when the 5 p.m. bell rings. To them work is a chore and they are willing to expend only the minimum necessary effort in accomplishing it. To achieve high motivation there needs to be a rough match between personal and organisational aims and it is this match that many 'motivation' schemes seek to achieve. For years managers have debated what brings about high motivation, with some managers still believing that clean toilets and works outings are the key to success whilst others believe that meaningful participation in decision making or co-ownership are the answers. But all agree that motivation is very, very important and without it any organisation undertaking teambuilding would be wasting its time and resources because people would not be prepared to put in the necessary time and effort.

LOW CREATIVITY

How creative people are depends on a whole range of things, not least of all high motivation and freedom from bureaucratic controls. Teambuilding can play an important part in originating the kind of climate in which creativity can flourish, but it is not solely a question of teamwork. In particular, people need to know that ideas will be welcomed and valued. The signs of low creativity are easily recognisable, for example, empty suggestion boxes, dull meetings, lack of new products, yesterday's practices, and competitors having all the new development ideas. Lack of creativity can partly be caused by poor teamwork but it can also have at its root wrong people, restrictive management or simply too much concern for the present and too little for the future.

INAPPROPRIATE MANAGEMENT PHILOSOPHY

Management philosophy starts at the top. If the top managers in an organisation hold views about people at work which prevent management being exercised in an open, honest and supportive manner then real teamwork is unlikely to get off the ground. We may take, as an example, a particular teambuilding assignment in a factory where the 'top man' presented the problem of his managers not working effectively together. He saw bickering and hostility towards each other but they had a very different view. Individually, they said that the top man worked on the 'divide and rule' principle, believing that his managers needed constant threats to motivate them and by his own actions he destroyed any chances of teamwork. In short, they felt that his beliefs about people and the way he acted these out were alien to the principles of effective teamwork. Happily, a few months later, the seeds of real teamwork were beginning to germinate in that organisation but the main factor which brought that about was a change in the basic assumptions and beliefs of that 'top man'. The project turned out to be one which was really about helping him as an individual to manage people in a different way, motivating rather than demotivating.

LACK OF SUCCESSION PLANNING AND DEVELOPMENT

These problems are really a step further on from those of recruitment and selection. People need to grow with the firm and systematically take on bigger responsibilities. If they do not, then inevitably there will be a shortage of people of the right calibre to staff key positions. Effective teamwork is important throughout an organisation but it is critical at management level and without management succession and development the organisation will be without the raw material for a really effective top management team.

UNCLEAR AIMS

Teams exist to undertake tasks, and without a task no team has a basis for existence. It necessarily follows that any organisation wishing to build effective teams needs a clear view of where it wants to go and why. Highly developed teams without an aim will quickly degenerate and groups of people without a task will never be able to practise true teamwork.

UNFAIR REWARDS

In an organisation the way people are valued is largely shown by the rewards given to them, and unless people are of independent means then pay is by far the most important part of the reward package. However, there are other more subtle rewards which an organisation can confer on its staff. Holidays, cars, offices, even secretaries are seen by many as very important rewards. There are also many subtle punishments which organisations can hand out to those whose contribution is not so valued. Almost everyone feels underpaid and undervalued at some time especially when they see others, whose worth to the organisation they would put lower than their own, receiving a better 'reward package' than themselves. I have never yet seen a totally equitable reward system but the really gaping sores of inequitable rewards should be tackled before effective teamwork can flourish. In the words of the old saying, 'if you pay peanuts you get monkeys', ... and by contrast today's organisations need to be staffed by effective teams of men and women.

The above list may seem formidable and managers would be correct in taking the view that if all of them needed to be right before effective teamwork could commence then the idea would be better forgotten. Effective teamwork is linked to all of them because they are all about people and the things they do in organisations and any work on teambuilding will usually lead us also into those areas. Anyone contemplating teambuilding has to realise that effective teamwork is just one of the factors which lead to organisational health and whilst it can make a major contribution it will not solve all the 'people problems' which are commonly found in organisations.

NOTE

[1] M. Woodcock and D. Francis, *People at Work – A Practical Guide to Organisational Change*, University Associates, La Jolla, California, 1975.

4
Diagnosing teamwork problems

Debates about what constitutes an effective team can be endless but, as we saw in Chapter 1, most such teams seem to exhibit a set of common characteristics, characteristics which are associated with the mature team. These were referred to as the building blocks of effective teamwork:

1   Clear objectives and agreed goals.
2   Openness and confrontation.
3   Support and trust.
4   Co-operation and conflict.
5   Sound procedures.
6   Appropriate leadership.
7   Regular review.
8   Individual development.
9   Sound inter-group relations.

The following questionnaire enables us to look at team strengths and weaknesses under each of these headings. Using it will start the process of diagnosing teamwork problems and of understanding the concepts involved.

THE BUILDING BLOCKS QUESTIONNAIRE

This simple questionnaire has been developed as an aid to discovering which of the nine building blocks of effective teamwork could be most useful to your team. It is a collection of statements which team members might be heard to make about affairs in their team and the more people in the team who complete it the more accurate will be the results.

It is important to ensure that those completing it share a common perception of who comprises the team under review, as, of course, some may see themselves as belonging to more than one team.

At the end of Part I (pages 49–51) there is a section called 'Selecting Teambuilding Activities' which indicates those particular activities which can be used for exploring and using the building blocks. With the help of this questionnaire you can, therefore, not only get a quick indication of which building blocks to use in your team but also be directed to those activities which will most easily start to make the team more effective.

Instructions for completion
1 Turn to the answer grid on p. 27.
2 Work through the statements, in numerical order, marking an 'X' on the appropriate square of the grid if you think a statement about *your* team is broadly true. If you think a statement is not broadly true, leave the square blank.
3 Do not spend a great deal of time considering each statement; a few seconds should be long enough.
4 Remember that the results will be worthwhile only if you are truthful.

'BUILDING BLOCKS' QUESTIONNAIRE

1   Decisions seem to be forced upon us.
2   People are not encouraged to speak out.
3   When the going gets tough it is every man for himself.
4   Communication needs improving.
5   Decisions are taken at the wrong level.
6   Some of the managers are not true to themselves.
7   We seldom question the content or usefulness of our meetings.
8   Insufficient development opportunities are created.
9   We are frequently at loggerheads with other departments.
10 No one is really clear where we are going.
11 People do not say what they really think.
12 People have an 'I'm all right Jack' attitude.
13 Conflict is destructive in this team.
14 There is inadequate information on which to base decisions.
15 Some of the managers are not trusted.
16 We do not learn from our mistakes.
17 Managers do not help their subordinates to learn.
18 Relationships with other groups are 'cool'.
19 We are all very busy but we do not seem to get anywhere.
20 Issues are brushed under the carpet.
21 It would help if people were more willing to admit their mistakes.
22 There is mistrust and hostility.
23 People are uncommitted to decisions.
24 There is little team loyalty.
25 Outside opinions are unwelcome.
26 There should be more job rotation.
27 We seldom work effectively with other teams.
28 We do not spend adequate time planning for the future.
29 Delicate issues are avoided.
30 People get 'stabbed in the back'.
31 We do not really work together.
32 Inappropriate people make the decisions.
33 Managers are weak and not prepared to stand up and be counted.
34 I do not receive sufficient feedback.
35 The wrong kinds of skills are developed.
36 Help is not forthcoming from other parts of the organisation.

37   We do not have a clear view of what is expected of us.
38   Honesty is not a feature of our team.
39   I do not feel strengthened by my colleagues.
40   Skills and information are not shared sufficiently.
41   It is the strong personalities that get their own way.
42   Dignity is not recognised.
43   We should spend more time questionning the way we operate.
44   Managers do not take personal development seriously.
45   The rest of the organisation does not understand us.
46   The way an individual is valued has little to do with what he achieves.
47   There are too many secrets.
48   Conflicts are avoided.
49   Disagreements fester.
50   Commitment to decisions is low.
51   Our manager(s) believe(s) that tighter supervision produces increased results.
52   There are too many taboos in this team.
53   There are manifestly better opportunities in other departments.
54   We put a lot of energy into defending our boundaries.
55   Priorities are unclear.
56   People are not involved sufficiently in decision-making.
57   There are too many recriminations.
58   There is not enough listening.
59   We do not utilise the skills we have available.
60   Managers believe that people are inherently lazy.
61   We spend too much time doing and not enough thinking.
62   Individuals are not encouraged to grow.
63   We do not try to understand the views of other teams.
64   We do not understand what other departments are aiming at.
65   Some people back down too easily.
66   Generally there is low trust here.
67   People are unwilling to take the views of others into account.
68   We do not consider alternative solutions sufficiently.
69   Yesterday's attitudes prevail with our manager(s).
70   The accepted order is rarely challenged.
71   Our manager(s) back(s) the skills to develop others.
72   We have too little influence on the rest of the organisation.
73   Managers do not plan for the future together.
74   In this team it pays to keep your mouth shut.
75   A lot of time is spent 'defining' territory.

76   There are too many fights.
77   People feel frustrated because they are not consulted.
78   Management does not care whether people are happy in their work.
79   We seldom change our working procedures or organisation.
80   We should spend more time growing our own senior people.
81   We do not reach out to help other groups.
82   Different parts of the organisation are pulling in different directions.
83   People are not prepared to put their true beliefs on the table.
84   People are not really helped to develop.
85   This place reminds me of a battlefield sometimes.
86   There is a need for more democracy.
87   Managers take little action to make employees' jobs interesting and meaningful.
88   Delicate issues are not raised.
89   Many people trained by the company later join competitors.
90   Ideas from outside the team are not used.
91   Our aims are not democratically agreed.
92   Team members do not get sufficient honest feedback.
93   People should stand on their own feet more.
94   We should discuss our differences more.
95   Team members are not sufficiently involved in taking decisions.
96   Our leader does not make the best use of us.
97   We should seriously consider the relevance of our meetings.
98   Individual development is stifled by the team.
99   Information does not flow freely enough between teams.
100   We should place more emphasis on 'results'.
101   People 'hear what they want to hear' rather than the truth.
102   More time should be devoted to discussing fundamental values.
103   We do not get down to the root of our differences.
104   Decisions are taken at the wrong level.
105   Our leader is not true to his own beliefs.
106   We should take more account of how others see us.
107   People are discouraged from being authentic.
108   The organisation as a whole is not a happy place to work in.

'BUILDING BLOCKS' ANSWER SHEET

Follow the instructions given at the beginning of the questionnaire. In the grid there are 108 squares, each one numbered to correspond to a question. Mark an 'X' through the square if you think a statement about your organisation is broadly true. If you think a statement is not broadly true, leave the square blank. Fill in the top line first, working from left to right; then fill in the second and subsequent lines. Be careful not to miss a question.

A	B	C	D	E	F	G	H	I
1	2	3	4	5	6	7	8	9
10	11	12	13	14	15	16	17	18
19	20	21	22	23	24	25	26	27
28	29	30	31	32	33	34	35	36
37	38	39	40	41	42	43	44	45
46	47	48	49	50	51	52	53	54
55	56	57	58	59	60	61	62	63
64	65	66	67	68	69	70	71	72
73	74	75	76	77	78	79	80	81
82	83	84	85	86	87	88	89	90
91	92	93	94	95	96	97	98	99
100	101	102	103	104	105	106	107	108
Totals								

When you have considered all 108 statements, total the number of Xs in each vertical column and turn to the next page.

Now write the scores for each column here.

A		This is the score for Clear objectives and agreed goals
B		Openness and confrontation
C		Support and trust
D		Co-operation and conflict
E		Sound working and decision-making procedures
F		Appropriate leadership
G		Regular review
H		Individual development
I		Sound inter-group relations

The building blocks with the highest scores are the ones which you could use most profitably to bring improvements to your team. In Part II there is a lecturette on each one of these building blocks which will explain it in greater depth. Before undertaking any team development activity you should study those which relate to your highest scoring blocks. At the end of Part I is a key which links the collection of practical activities in Part II with these building blocks. By using it you can select those teambuilding activities which are appropriate to your team right now.

However, before you rush to try them you should work through the rest of Part I. This will help you avoid many of the pitfalls and barriers you could easily come across.

5
Action planning

Action planning is vital if your teambuilding efforts are to succeed. It also needs to be part of a simple framework which includes identification of needs and subsequent review of action. In any development activity the simple framework shown below should always be kept in mind.

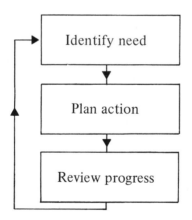

Simple action-planning framework

It is not advisable to start action planning until you have identified a need and always review progress during and after the action. Action planning can be as simple as following the checklist of questions given below, an approach which will help ensure that:

    needs are identified;

    needs are agreed;

the right people are involved;
action is practical and appropriate;
the right resources are used;
other implications are considered;
the right time scale is adopted;
results are used as a basis for further improvement.

SIMPLE CHECKLIST APPROACH TO ACTION PLANNING

Some typical examples are listed below each question.

1 *What is the need?*
To improve openness.
To develop a more effective form of leadership.
To improve our decision-making ability.
To clarify our objectives.
To generally review and improve the way we operate
as a team.

2 *Is this need agreed by those affected?*
Has everyone been consulted?
Have we ensured commitment?
Do we have to spend more time agreeing needs?

3 *To whom does it apply?*
The whole team.
Leaders of different teams.
Task groups.
An individual.

4 *How will we know if we have been successful?*
Are we sure of our development objectives?
Are they measurable?
Can other people help us to evaluate?
What behavioural changes do we expect?

5 *Is anyone else likely to be affected?*
Other teams or departments.
The organisation as a whole.
Other team leaders.
Do we need approval?

6   *What methods, techniques or actions shall we adopt?*
The teambuilding activities in this manual.
Other activities and techniques known to me.
Other sources of ideas.

7   *What other resources will we need?*
Are we (or I) competent to undertake the activities?
Do we need external help?
Can other departments or teams help us?
Do we need to get out of the work situation?

8   *What time scale shall we adopt?*
1 month
1 year

9   *How shall we review progress?*
By self review.
By process observation.
By regular specific review meetings.
By other review methods contained in this book.

10   *How will we assess whether further action is necessary?*
Should we evaluate our effect on others?
Should we analyse our needs again?

6
Groundrules for team development

People who have implemented teamwork improvement programmes generally have a great many 'war stories' to tell. Many mistakes have been made but from them it is possible to draw up some groundrules which should steer you away from many of the pitfalls and potential disaster areas. Most of them can be avoided if these simple rules are followed.

Start modestly. Remember that big oaks from little acorns grow and avoid grand designs. Success builds success and people will be much more committed to your ideas if they have seen some simple things bringing improvement. It is invariably better to start with a topic which can be easily grasped.

Be clear about your aims. It is often said that providing a group of intelligent individuals know what they want to achieve they will usually be capable of finding a way of achieving it. So often people seem to lose sight of the aim or become more concerned with the method than with the outcome.

Remember that the unknown is usually more threatening than the known. Hardy, the trusted companion of Lord Nelson, on leaving the sea took up a post at the Greenwich Naval College near London. The story is told of him as a local dignitary receiving an invitation to be a passenger on the first passenger railway train from Greenwich to Central London. Hardy, a man who had fought gallantly in some of the most bloody and horrendous sea battles in history, declined the invitation as 'he could see little point in exposing himself to the tremendous risks involved'.

Remember that development is basically self-regulated. Limitations are imposed by age, beliefs and capacity, and although you can create development opportunities ultimately individuals are responsible for their own development.

Remember those who have not had development opportunities. Successful development for some can mean jealousy from others who may feel aggrieved at not being part of the action.

Be alive to other opportunities which your actions may create. Working on teamwork issues will inevitably bring about opportunities to improve such things as individual development, the flow of ideas in the organisation, etc., and as a team becomes more effective it will begin to challenge things such as the way you are organised, the salary system, recruitment policies. All of these can be either barriers to your success or opportunities for greater success. The wise man uses opportunities well.

Ensure that you have the agreement of participants before you proceed. Commitment to change comes from real understanding of the process you are about to embark upon. It may seem on occasions that you have to spend three times as much energy explaining to people what it is you are about to do as on the action itself, but no changes will be beneficial in the long run if they lack the commitment of those whom they affect.

Remember you can take a horse to water but you cannot make it drink. People cannot be forced into changing their attitudes. They need to make up their own minds about where they stand and about what seems right to them. Similarly, you cannot force people to be open and honest. You may be able to force them to pretend to be open and to say they are honest but no good will come from inducing people to act contrary to their beliefs.

Be ready to accept the need for external help on occasions. Whilst taking responsibility for your own actions and helping others to do the same, there are many advantages that can be gained by using an 'outsider' in your organisation. If you choose wisely you can capitalise upon the advantages of his impartiality and lack of vested interest by, for instance, asking him to observe your everyday meetings. But do not be afraid to question his approach, experience and beliefs. Such action is likely to increase his respect for you.

Learn from your mistakes. Always be ready to admit you are wrong and use your past experience as a guide to improve future action. This means regular reviewing of the targets you have set and encouraging others to do the same. Honest feedback is the most valuable thing which your colleagues can give to you but people will not give honest feedback if they think that it will not be welcomed and may be used against them.

Consult widely and genuinely. People really do have a useful contribution to make and having been consulted they will also feel more committed to the project. It is easy to look upon consultation as a chore, or as a subtle way of selling an idea, and many managers are well practised in the skill of persuading others. However, manipulation of this kind is likely to undermine any teambuilding effort.

Face up to 'political' or organisational problems. Every organisation has its politics and its politicians and turning a blind eye to them will not make them go away. Try to recognise the political barriers at an early stage, take account of them in your plans and, if necessary, confront them squarely and openly. Above all do not play the political game yourself; this will only discredit you in the eyes of those you are trying to help.

Encourage frank discussions about principles and practice. Deep rooted prejudices, views and beliefs will only change if they are brought into the open and explored at length. Never stifle discussion, you will have a healthier organisation if team members are accustomed to discussing matters of principle in a constructive way. Remember that you will be taking people into the unknown and everyone is naturally apprehensive about things they do not understand or which seem to herald major changes. In addition, as the team increases its skill and experience, it will become increasingly willing and able to deal with more difficult problems.

Keep your plans and actions related to the work of the organisation. People are unlikely to experiment if that experimentation involves substantial extra work. One good way of adhering to this rule is to try to use meetings and current projects as the basis for any improvement. The more work related you can keep your plans the more people will be willing to try them and the easier it will be to see meaningful results.

Be realistic about time scales. Rome was not built in a day, and you are unlikely to see any overnight changes. The way in which people behave in organisations is often the result of a lifetime's learning and whenever older people embark on new organisational learning there is a lot of 'unlearning' which needs to accompany it. Change in the culture of an organisation is something which is very difficult to achieve. It requires constant attention and must be spread over a realistic time scale.

Do not raise expectations which you cannot meet. It is easy to promise people that any activities you embark upon will bring whole-sale benefits but both you and the designs will be discredited if those around you are able to see clearly that your schemes did not really succeed. It is therefore imperative to be alive to, and to face up to, organisational and political problems and to recognise that for every two steps forward which you take you may also have to take one backwards.

Delegate where appropriate. There may be particular development activities which you are not well suited to undertake. In these circumstances look around for others who may be better equipped, remembering that delegation itself is one of the best development opportunities you are likely to find.

Re-organise or re-allocate work when necessary. People cannot always cope with their existing responsibilities as well as development prospects.

Practise what you preach. You will be judged by your actions much more than by your words.

A final note of caution. Although your efforts may bring results remember that your success can lead to problems for others in terms of

- Improving the effectiveness of your team can make other, less productive groups feel insecure.
- People and teams can and do grow beyond the needs of their present roles.
- The new methods of working which your team will develop can easily challenge the style and operation of the whole organisation.
- Jealousy and resentment can be created in those who have not been part of the action.

7
Designing teambuilding events

The material in this manual has been set out in a way which will enable those who wish to facilitate work on teambuilding to use it to design training and intervention programmes. For instance the theory included in Part II has been grouped into nine brief and concise lecturettes in order that they can easily be used as 'inputs', 'handouts' or 'aide mémoires'. Similarly the techniques, structured experiences, methods and questionnaires, called activities, are presented in a format which enables them to be used by the facilitator in either a training session or an everyday work situation. I have also tried as far as possible to link each of the activities with the theory, particularly by identifying those activities which can be used to explore further the various 'building blocks of effective teamwork'.

In order to help further those who wish to build up training or intervention designs a number of example designs have been included which I have personally used and which have been built up entirely from the contents of this manual. The designs are flexible and can be adjusted to suit different participants, problems and time scales. It is hoped that they will be useful in demonstrating the way in which the material in the book can be used to build up training sessions. This can be done by using a set of simple guidelines, which, if followed, should be of great assistance in designing training events which are stimulating, meaningful and enjoyable.

GUIDELINES FOR DESIGNING TRAINING EVENTS

1   Always start by defining the objectives you wish to achieve.

2   Select activities and lecturettes which will best help you achieve the objectives.

3   Establish a timetable and keep to it as far as possible. Make sure that other facilitators or leaders understand the time constraints.

4   As far as possible select and use activities which reinforce the points made in the lecturettes.

5   Try to intersperse activities, lecturettes and discussions to give a balanced programme.

6   Allow adequate time to discuss or process the activities.

7   Use only activities which you feel you can handle efficiently given the facilities and help which are available to you.

8   Try to start with an 'unfreezing' activity which will not be seen as threatening and will allow people to immediately begin participating in the event.

9   Try out activities with which you are not familiar *before* the event.

10   Ensure that adequate preparation is done before the event begins. In particular, check that answer sheet, copies of activities and visual aids are to hand.

11   Consider how structured you wish the event to be.

In the main, heavily structured events are easier to handle, particularly for managers and trainers who may be breaking new ground. Because of this they stand a greater chance of achieving their objectives, and of giving their participants a greater feeling of security.

In less structured events, where participants are given more opportunity to influence the content and style, there is greater scope for real and deep learning because participants are more likely to learn from their own participation. A more flexible design will give more options and freedom and allow participants to resolve issues which are peculiar to them. However, greater skill is usually required from the trainer.

Often trainers build their experience and ability by moving from more to less structured events.

12   Try to eliminate jargon and difficult theory wherever possible.

13   Remember that most of the activities in Part II are capable of amendment to satisfy your own particular requirements.

14   The event will have a greater chance of success if the participants have themselves been involved in defining the problem.

THE TRAINING DESIGNS

The different designs which can be derived from the material are almost endless. A few examples are given to show how the material can be arranged for different purposes, though not to suggest actual designs for use by the reader who is strongly advised to build up his own designs using the guidelines given earlier. Therefore, training designs which vary in objectives, in length and in participants have been purposely included.

1: Improving our teamwork
Originally designed as a 'starter' event to enable an existing team to explore the potential of, and need for, teambuilding. I have often used this design with teams who are considering teamwork for the first time and need a general introduction as a prelude to further work.

2: An introduction to team leadership issues
Designed to allow managers with no previous experience of teambuilding activities to begin examining their own role and behaviour in relation to the teams they are leading. Originally used with managers in a large organisation who had previously received no formal training, it has been used since to whet the appetite of many managers.

3: An introduction to teamwork
An introduction to team development for people who do not regularly work together and wish to be introduced to its potential. Originally it was used for a large gathering of chief executives of retail stores groups who had heard about team development and wanted to know a little more.

4: Teamwork workshop
A medium length event enabling people to familiarise themselves with essential theory and activities as a prelude to understanding teambuilding activities in their own teams/organisations. The design has been used on several occasions as the basis for public workshops

where trainers and managers from different organisations come together for two to three days.

5: Improving my management of others

A full day in which managers can assess their performance as team leaders and make plans to improve their future performance. A step on from design 2 this can be used where managers are prepared to invest a full day in examining their own strengths and weaknesses. This design was originally put together for a group of managers, each of whom managed individual plants, who met together for an annual business conference and wished to spend part of the time examining how they managed their own units.

6: Depth teambuilding workshop

A one week event in which a team can work seriously on the fundamental issues which will improve its functioning and prepare plans for the future.

7: Understanding teamwork

A one day event for those who need to understand the theory of team development but who do not regularly work together. The design was originally used with a group of consultants who had little experience of teambuilding but were increasingly being asked by clients to advise on its potential.

EXAMPLE TRAINING DESIGN 1: IMPROVING OUR TEAMWORK

Objectives
To provide an opportunity for teams to understand:
(a)   The importance of teamwork.
(b)   Its relationship to other organisational problems.
(c)   The need for improvement.

Time required: Approximately 1 day.

Participants: Teams who regularly work together and have not previously been exposed to teambuilding theory or activities.

Programme Item	Approximate time required	Source
1 Lecturette 'What is teamwork?' (preceded by Brainstorming)	50 min	Part I Section 1 Activity 13
2 Distribution of 'Building blocks' questionnaire Completion of 'Building blocks' questionnaire (facilitator collects)	30 min	Part I Section 4
3 Activity 'Highway Code'	60 min	Activity 25
4 Review of performance in 'Highway Code' (Group discussion)	40 min	
LUNCH		
5 Activity 'Zin obelisk' followed by review	40 min	Activity 31
6 Lecturette 'Stages of development'	30 min	Part I Section 2
7 Activity 'Our team and its stage of development'	30 min	Activity 1
8 Results of 'Building blocks' questionnaire presented by facilitator Discussion of results	50 min	
9 Lecturette 'What teamwork will not do'	30 min	Part I Section 3

EXAMPLE TRAINING DESIGN 2: AN INTRODUCTION TO TEAM LEADERSHIP ISSUES

Objectives
To provide an opportunity for team leaders to:
(a) Question their assumptions and beliefs about the management of others.
(b) Examine their performance in working with others.

Time required: Approximately 4 hours.

Participants: Anyone with responsibility for the leadership/management of groups.

Programme

Item	Source
1 *Our assumptions and beliefs*	
Completion of 'Team leadership style'	
questionnaire	Activity 7
Lecturette 'Appropriate leadership'	Lecturette 6
Sharing of results and discussion	
2 *Working with others*	
Task 1 'Zin obelisk'	Activity 31
Lecturette 'What makes teams effective'	Lecturettes 1–9
	(précis in Part I)
Task 2 'Team rating'	Activity 3
Discussion of results	
Task 3 'My meetings with others'	Activity 9

EXAMPLE TRAINING DESIGN 3: AN INTRODUCTION TO TEAMWORK

Objectives
To provide a basic introduction to teamwork issues by:
(a) Explaining *basic* teamwork theory.
(b) Experiencing simple teamwork activities.

Time required: Approximately 3 hours.

Participants: Anyone who has not experienced teambuilding activities previously.

Programme

Item	Source
1 Task 1 'Cave rescue'	Activity 27
2 Lecturette 'What is teamwork?'	Part I
'Characteristics of effective	
teamwork'	Lecturettes 1–9
	(précis in Part I)
3 Discussion – Teams review performance in	
Task 1 against 'Team self-review'	Activity 41
4 Task 2 'Highway Code'	Activity 25
5 Discussion – Teams review performance in	
Task 2 against 'Team self-review'	Activity 41

EXAMPLE TRAINING DESIGN 4: TEAMWORK WORKSHOP

Objectives
To provide a medium length training experience in which participants can:
(a) Explore the importance of effective teamwork.
(b) Understand basic teamwork theory.
(c) Consider particularly issues of management style, support and trust, co-operation and conflict.
(d) Receive practical guidance and ideas on assessing teamwork problems and beginning to improve teamwork.
(e) Develop action plans based on the above.

Time required: 2 days.

Participants: Key managers in an organisation.

Programme

	Item	Approximate time required	Source
Day 1			
1	Activity 'To see ourselves as others see us' and discussion of results	60 min	Activity 38
2	Activity 'Highway Code'	60 min	Activity 25
3	Lecturette 'What is teamwork?' (co-operation and conflict, support and trust, and appropriate leadership are identified as basis for rest of design)	45 min	Part I Section 1
4	Syndicates review performance against criteria outlined	45 min	
LUNCH			
5	Lecturette 'Co-operation and conflict'	10 min	Lecturette 4
	Activity 'Prisoners' dilemma' with	60 min	Activity 29
	Activity 'Process review'	25 min	Activity 39
6	Lecturette 'Support and trust'	10 min	Lecturette 3
	Activity 'Cave rescue'	45 min	Activity 27
	Activity 'Team self-review'	25 min	Activity 41
7	Lecturette 'Appropriate leadership'	10 min	Lecturette 6

EXAMPLE TRAINING DESIGN 4: TEAMWORK WORKSHOP
(Continued)

7   (continued)
     Activity 'Team leadership style'   40 min   Activity 7

BREAK

8   Activity 'Human structure'   45 min   Activity 30
     Activity 'Four letter words'   45 min   Activity 33

Day 2

1   Lecturette 'Individual development'   15 min   Lecturette 8
     Activity 'Characteristics of   20 min   Activity 8
     personal effectiveness'
     Discussion of results in pairs   30 min
2   Distribution and individual
     completion of 'Building blocks'
     questionnaire   25 min   Part I Section 4
     Analysis and presentation of results   25 min
3   Action planning: Participants   120 min   Part I
     prepare plans for improvement
     of teamwork in back home
     situation using (a) personal
     learning achieved in workshop,
     (b) other activities from *Team*   Part II
     Development Manual,
     (c) action planning section   Part I
4   Teams present action plans   60 min
5   Lecturette 'Groundrules for   30 min   Part I Section 6
     team development'

EXAMPLE TRAINING DESIGN 5: IMPROVING MY MANAGEMENT OF OTHERS

Objectives
To provide an opportunity for managers to:
(a) Question their assumptions and beliefs about the management of others.
(b) Assess their personal performance in working with others.
(c) Obtain basic guidance on applying this learning in their own situation.

Time required: 1 day.

Participants: Managers who normally lead teams.

Programme

	Source
1 *My assumptions and beliefs about others* Completion of 'Management style: Theory X–Y'	Activity 20
Lecturette 'Appropriate leadership'	Lecturette 6
Discussion on lecturette content and results of questionnaire	
2 *My performance in working with others* Activity 'The Zin obelisk'	Activity 31
Review of results (processors may be used) (or team self review)	Activity 39 or 41
Lecturette 'What is teamwork?'	Part I Section 1
Activity 'My meetings with others'	Activity 9
3 *My performance as a coach* Activity 'How good a coach are you?'	Activity 17
4 *My overall performance* Activity 'Team leader effectiveness'	Activity 6
5 Action planning with (a) Groundrules for team development	Part I Section 6
(b) Action planning checklist	Part I Section 5
(c) 'Being a better coach'	Activity 18
(d) Group counselling by facilitator	

EXAMPLE TRAINING DESIGN 6: DEPTH TEAMBUILDING WORKSHOP

Objectives
To provide an opportunity for team members to:
(a) Understand the importance of teamwork.
(b) Relate this to operational plans.
(c) Analyse team development needs.
(d) Prepare action plans for teamwork improvement.

Time required: 5 days.

Participants: Intact work group or leaders of a number of teams.

Programme

Day 1	Source
1 Presentation of forward work-plans for organisation or work group and agreement of them	

Day 2 Understanding teamwork

2 Activity 'Who are you?'	Activity 23
3 Activity 'Highway Code'	Activity 25
4 Lecturette 'What is teamwork?'	Part I Section 1
'Team self-review' briefing followed by review of performance in 'Highway Code'	Activity 41
5 Lecturette 'Co-operation and conflict'	Lecturette 4
Activity 'Prisoners' dilemma'	Activity 29
Activity 'Process review'	Activity 39
6 Lecturette 'Support and trust'	Lecturette 3
7 Activity 'Cave rescue'	Activity 27
Activity 'Process review'	Activity 39

Day 3

7 Lecturette 'Appropriate leadership'	Lecturette 6
Activity 'Management style: theory X–Y'	Activity 20
8 Activity 'Characteristics of personal effectiveness'	Activity 8
Lecturette 'Individual development'	Lecturette 8
Dyads discuss results of 'Characteristics of personal effectiveness'	

Day 3 (continued)	Source
9 Lecturette 'Clear objectives'	Lecturette 1
Activity 'Four letter words'	Activity 33
10 Lecturette 'Decision-making'	Lecturette 5
Activity 'How we take decisions'	Activity 45

(In activities where process review is used members should take turns acting as observer. The facilitators may deliver a brief lecturette on process review *either* in plenary session *or* repeated to each group of observers as they take turns.)

Day 4

11 Lecturette 'The stages of team development'	Part I Section 2
Activity 'Our team and its stage of development'	Activity 1
12 Completion of 'Building blocks' questionnaire	Part I
Lecturette 'Building blocks of effective teamwork'	Lecturettes 1–9 (précis Part I)
13 Discussion of results	
14 Lecturette 'Action planning'	Part I (Action Planning and groundrules for team development)

Day 5 Action planning

15 Participants split into small groups to prepare actions plans for:
    (a)   Individual development
    (b)   Group development

    Use as basis for planning:

    (a)   Results of
         'Characteristics of personal effectiveness'
         'Management style: Theory X–Y'
         Choosing building blocks
         'Our team and its stage of development'
    (b)   Discussions after each activity including
         'Process Review' and 'Team self-review'
    (c)   Copies of all activities in Part II which are distributed

16 Plans of small groups presented to all participants
17 General discussion, comment on plans, and review of event

EXAMPLE TRAINING DESIGN 7: TEAMWORK ISSUES

Objectives
To promote understanding of Team development theory.

Time required: 1 day.

Participants: Groups or individuals who need to understand the basics.
They need not normally work together.

Programme

		Approximate time required	Source
1	Pre-work – completion of Steps 1-4 'Team effectiveness action plan'		Activity 12
2	Choosing building blocks	30 min	Part I
3	Activity 'The Zin obelisk'	25 min	Activity 31
	Review by 'Process review'	30 min	Activity 39
	Discussion: The characteristics of effective teamwork	30 min	
4	Lecturette 'The building blocks of effective teamwork'	20 min	Lecturettes 1–9 (précis Part I) Explanation 4
	Activity 'Intimacy exercise' (openness and confrontation)	30 min	Activity 24
	Activity 'Silent shapes' (co-operation and conflict)	30 min	Activity 42
	Review by 'Team self-review'	20 min	Activity 41
	Activity 'Positive and negative feedback' (support and trust)	30 min	Activity 36
5	Choosing building blocks (results)	30 min	
	Activity 'Team rating'	25 min	Activity 3
6	Lecturette 'Stages of team development'	15 min	Part I Section 2
	Activity 'Our team and its stage of development'	20 min	Activity 1
7	Completion of step 6 'Team effectiveness action plan'	30 min	Activity 12

8
Selecting teambuilding activities

On the following pages you will find a key to the collection of resources which have been assembled in Part II. There are two kinds of resources – activities and lecturettes. Each individual activity contains a statement of purpose, but this guide is intended to line up the activities with the lecturettes. By so doing it identifies which activities can be used to help understand and bring about:

(a) clear objectives;
(b) openness and confrontation;
(c) support and trust;
(d) co-operation and conflict;
(e) sound working and decision-making procedures;
(f) appropriate leadership;
(g) regular review;
(h) individual development;
(i) sound inter-group relations.

These of course are the nine 'building blocks' of effective teamwork referred to earlier. In the same way it also identifies which lecturettes can be used to help understanding of the issues raised by each activity.

Activities	Sound inter-group relations	Individual development	Regular review	Appropriate leadership	Sound procedures	Co-operation and conflict	Support and trust	Openness and confrontation	Clear objectives
1 Our team and its stage of development		*	*	*	*	*	*	*	*
2 What makes teams effective?	*	*	*		*				
3 Team rating	*	*	*						
4 The teams in my working life	*	*							
5 Team mirroring			*				*	*	
6 Team leader effectiveness	*	*		*					
7 Team leadership style		*	*	*					
8 Characteristics of personal effectiveness		*	*	*	*				
9 My meetings with others		*			*				
10 Use of time		*		*	*				*
11 Force field analysis		*			*			*	*
12 Team effectiveness action plan			*					*	*
13 Brainstorming		*			*			*	
14 Team openness exercise					*				
15 Review and appraisal meetings				*					
16 Enlivening meetings			*	*					*
17 How good a coach are you?		*		*					
18 Being a better coach		*		*					
19 Counselling to increase learning		*		*					

	1	2	3	4	5	6	7	8	9
20 Management style		*		*		*	*	*	
21 Discussing values						*	*	*	
22 Team member development needs		*							
23 Who are you?	*	*						*	
24 Intimacy exercise	*						*		
25 Highway Code	*			*		*	*	*	*
26 Is the team listening?	*	*							
27 Cave rescue						*			
28 Initial review			*				*	*	*
29 Prisoners' dilemma	*			*		*	*	*	*
30 Human structure			*	*				*	*
31 The Zin obelisk	*			*	*	*			*
32 Clover leaf	*			*	*				*
33 Four letter words	*		*		*			*	*
34 Team tasks	*		*	*	*	*	*	*	*
35 Making meetings more constructive	*		*	*			*	*	
36 Positive and negative feedback	*		*		*		*	*	
37 Improving one-to-one relationships	*	*			*	*	*		
38 To see ourselves as others see us	*		*		*			*	
39 Process review			*		*		*	*	
40 How we make decisions					*		*		
41 Team self-review			*						
42 Silent shapes			*		*				*
43 The working clock		*	*		*				*
44 Basic meeting arrangements			*	*	*				
45 Decision-taking				*	*				

PART II

TEAMBUILDING RESOURCES

Practical activities

All of the activities included here are useful and relevant to improving teamwork in a practical way. They are intended to be used in a flexible way to suit your particular needs and should be easily understood. To give detailed guidance on each activity would detract from this manual two of its distinguishing characteristics – conciseness and simplicity. Therefore, only activities which do not require elaborate explanation are included. However, as you select and use them remember the words of guidance in Part I, particularly 'Designing teambuilding events' and 'Groundrules for team development'.

Activity 1:
Our team and its stage of development

PURPOSE

To provide a simple structured way in which team members can consider the performance and stage of development of their own teams.

HOW TO DO IT

1   The facilitator gives an input based on Part I Section 2 'The stages of team development'.

2   The rating sheet (see overleaf) is distributed and participants are asked to reconsider the main characteristics of the four principal stages of development and to mark the rating scale where they consider their team to be.

3   The facilitator leads the group in a discussion which aims to:

(a) achieve consensus on the stage of development;

(b) formulate an agreed statement about the development needs of the group.

NOTES AND VARIATIONS

1   An alternative to an input is for participants to read Part I Section 2.

2   The activity may also be used to consider the stage of development of other teams from an outsider's viewpoint.

3   Completion of the activity by outsiders can be used to provide additional data for consideration by the team.

4   The activity can be used repeatedly throughout a planned programme of development to check progress and reassess needs.

5   The activity is particularly useful in bridging the gap between a consideration of theory and a commitment to action.

Rating sheet: Our team and its stage of development

Stage 1 Characteristics	Stage 2 Characteristics	Stage 3 Characteristics	Stage 4 Characteristics
1 Feelings not dealt with	1 Experimentation	Stage 2 with a more systematic approach	Stages 2 and 3 characteristics plus
2 The workplace is for work only	2 Risky issues debated, wider options debated	1 Methodical working	1 High flexibility
3 Established line prevails	3 Personal feelings raised	2 Agreed procedures	2 Appropriate leadership determined by situation
4 No 'rocking the boat'	4 More inward looking	3 Established groundrules	
5 Poor listening	5 Greater listening		3 Maximum use of energy and ability
6 Weakness covered up	6 More concern for others		
7 Unclear objectives	7 Sometimes uncomfortable		4 Basic principles considered, agreed and reviewed
8 Low involvement in planning			
9 Bureaucracy			5 Needs of all members met
10 Boss takes most decisions			6 Development a priority

```
┌───────────┬───────────┬───────────┐
```

Stage 1   Stage 2   Stage 3   Stage 4

Activity 2:
What makes teams effective?

To promote understanding of and agreement about 'the characteristics of effective teams'.

HOW TO DO IT

The facilitator explains that the team task is to rank the statements overleaf in order of importance by placing a (1) at the side of the most important, a (2) at the side of the second most important, etc., so that (9) appears alongside the least important statement.

NOTES AND VARIATIONS

1   Participants may be first asked to individually rank the statements before team ranking takes place.
2   The essential feature of the activity is the discussion which clarifies and aids understanding of each characteristic.
3   'What is teamwork?' in Part I may either be read or delivered as a lecturette before or after ranking.
4   Lecturettes 1–9 can be used to further explain each characteristic.
5   Participants may also be invited to add to the list of characteristics.

( ) The team is clear about what it wants to achieve.

( ) Issues are always confronted and dealt with in an open way.

( ) Members show support for each other and there is a high level of trust between them.

( ) Both co-operation and conflict are used to get the best results.

( ) There are sound and understood procedures for decision-making.

( ) Team leadership, where required, is of a high standard and in the most appropriate hands.

( ) The team regularly reviews the way it operates and learns from the experience.

( ) Individual and team development needs are regularly reviewed.

( ) Relations with other groups are sound.

Activity 3:
Team rating

To compare teams by assessing them against the characteristics which are commonly associated with success, and to help identify those teams which may be most in need of development, and provide a basis for helping them.

HOW TO DO IT

The activity can be undertaken by an individual, by a group representing a number of teams, or by a group who are not members of the teams to be rated.

1   Identify those teams which are to be reviewed.
2   The scoring sheet (see page 62) lists nine characteristics which successful teams invariably display. For each team reviewed, give marks out of ten for performance against each characteristic.
3   Compare results between teams and between criteria, asking particularly:
(a) Does this activity tell us anything about which teams are in need of development?
(b) Are there any criteria requiring attention and which are common to some/all teams reviewed?

NOTES AND VARIATIONS

1   Clearly the results will only be as valid as the perceptions of those taking part and care must be taken in reading too much into the

results. This is a good activity for starting discussion and *helping* to decide where to begin, but other indicators of performance should also be considered before any programme of action is undertaken.
2   The scale can also be used within a team to contrast the views of individual members.
3   As the headings are the same as for the building blocks questionnaire in Part I, this activity can easily be used in conjunction with it.
4   Lecturettes 1–9 can be used to explain each characteristic.

Team rating scoring sheet

	Team A	Team B	Team C	Team D	Team E	Total
Clear objectives and agreed goals						
Openness and confrontation						
Support and trust						
Co-operation and conflict						
Sound procedures						
Appropriate leadership						
Review						
Individual development						
Sound inter-group relations						
Total						

Activity 4:
The teams in my working life

PURPOSE

This activity helps to identify the various groups of teams to which we belong in our working lives and examines why some are more effective than others.

HOW TO DO IT

1 Consider four teams to which you belong and list them on a sheet of paper. Write a letter against each, beginning with A and continuing through to D. Do this before continuing with the next stage of the activity.

2 Continue by completing a check sheet (see opposite) for each group. Write the appropriate letter on each sheet.

When you have completed the check sheet look at the answers and record the letters which score:

1 or 2 on question 1	
5 or 6 on question 2	
1 or 2 on question 3	
5 or 6 on question 4	
1 or 2 on question 5	
5 or 6 on question 6	
1 or 2 on question 7	

Does this conform to your own experience of them?

CHECK SHEET
group letter

1 The group is effective   _____   The group is ineffective
   at getting things done   1 2 3 4 5 6   getting things done

2 Membership is vague   _____   Membership is defined
   and easy to achive   1 2 3 4 5 6   and difficult to achieve

3 The group has clear   _____   The group has little in-
   standards of behaviour   1 2 3 4 5 6   fluence on behaviour of
                                                        its members

4 There is no clear   _____   Individuals have clearly
   difference of roles   1 2 3 4 5 6   different roles in the
                                                        group

5 There are close per-   _____   Relationships are mainly
   sonal relationships   1 2 3 4 5 6   impersonal
   within the group

6 People share a clear   _____   People have a low under-
   concept of the   1 2 3 4 5 6   standing of group
   purpose of the group   purpose

7 People feel a strong   _____   There is little personal
   sence of personal   1 2 3 4 5 6   commitment to the
   commitment to the   group
   group

Now answer the following questions:

1 Which groups appear most often?
2 Which groups appear least often?
3 Which do you think are the most developed?
4 What has contributed to their development?
5 How could the least developed become more developed?

Activity 5:
Team mirroring

To see ourselves and our team as others see us. All of us form views of other groups of people. Sometimes these views are accurate, but often they act as a barrier to working together effectively. This barrier can sometimes be removed if we understand what we think about others and know what they think about us.

HOW TO DO IT

This activity needs two separate teams who normally work with or alongside each other. The process has been used successfully with such groups as top and middle managers, sales and production people, supervisors and operatives, teachers and students, and nurses and patients.

1   Introduce the activity to both teams with a short explanation of what is about to happen. Then separate the two groups and ask each to prepare a list of twenty-four adjectives, twelve positive and twelve negative, that best describe the other group. Choose a spokesman for each group to record the list of adjectives on a flip chart.

2   After 45 minutes both groups reunite and the spokesmen read and display their lists, and sum up their position by drawing attention to the key words. Everyone then considers the lists in silence for two minutes.

3   Participants divide into subgroups of four each, two from each team. Each subgroup takes approximately an hour to discuss how people see each other. In the last ten minutes, each person writes on a sheet of paper what he or she has learned from the exchange of views. These sheets, which remain anonymous, are collected and shared by the entire group.

4   Following this discussion some positive action should be agreed on, but if people cannot agree they should arrange to meet again.

NOTES AND VARIATIONS

1   Two, three or four groups can be used with each group receiving a list of adjectives from each other group.

2   The facilitator should make the point that, whether accurate or not, other people's perceptions are important and can act as real barriers to inter-group relationships.

3   Care should be taken when using boss/subordinate groupings as feedback is often more negative from subordinate groups.

4   Where teams from separate departments are used the feedback can be potentially threatening to management of the departments and care should be taken to 'pick up' the issues and turn them to productive use.

5   Activity 38 is similar in concept and more suitable for use as part of a training event.

Activity 6:
Team leader effectiveness

PURPOSE

To enable team leaders to assess their own effectiveness as leaders by self-appraisal.

HOW TO DO IT

1   The team leader assesses his own effectiveness on the team leader effectiveness sheet using a scale from 1–100 with 60 indicating satisfactory performance.
2   He discloses his assessment to one or more members of the team who comment on it.
3   He then reassesses his effectiveness in the light of comments received.
4   The cycle can be repeated.

NOTES AND VARIATIONS

1   The activity can be used as part of an appraisal process or as an aid in a coaching relationship.
2   A consideration of the issues raised in Lecturette 6 'Appropriate leadership' can be included. The activity is based on the characteristics of successful team leadership described in that lecturette.

Team leader effectiveness sheet

Using a scale from 0 to 100 (with 60 indicating satisfactory performance), rate yourself on the following items in terms of your effectiveness.

I am authentic and true to myself   _____

I am clear about the standards I wish to achieve   _____

I give and receive trust and loyalty   _____

I maintain the integrity and position of my team   _____

I am receptive to people's hopes, needs and
dignity   _____

I use delegation as an aid to achievement and
development   _____

I face facts honestly and squarely   _____

I encourage and assist personal and team
development   _____

I establish and maintain sound working
procedures   _____

I try to make work a happy and rewarding
place   _____

Activity 7:
Team leadership style

PURPOSE

Almost more than anything else, the way in which a team is led can affect the contribution and performance of those who work in it. This activity enables a team and its leader(s) to examine their assumptions about people and about management style. Based on McGregor's 'Theory X and Y' approach, it helps reveal what attitudes influence the team so that, brought into the open, these attitudes can be dealt with more effectively.

HOW TO DO IT

1   Ask the whole of the team to complete the leadership style questionnaire.
2   Ask for the questionnaires to be returned anonymously to a particular person by a certain date. The selected person then analyses the questionnaires and produces a chart showing the average leadership style which the team sees as prevailing (A), and the average preferred leadership style (B).
3   At a meeting of those who completed the questionnaire, the chart is shown and those present discuss the leadership styles, both perceived and preferred. Action is then identified which could improve leadership practice to the benefit of the whole team.

NOTES AND VARIATIONS

1   The activity can be conducted within a regular meeting or training event.
2   A lecturette on McGregor's 'Theory X and Y' model can be given

before or after completion. (An outline will be found in Lecturette 6: 'Appropriate leadership'.)

3   The co-operation of team leader(s) should always be forthcoming before this activity is tried.

LEADERSHIP STYLE QUESTIONNAIRE

The questionnaire is designed to identify the present leadership style in your team and your preferred leadership style. Read each question and place the letter 'A' over the number that most nearly represents the leadership attitudes that you feel are most commonly displayed. Then consider what you feel the attitude ought to be and indicate this with the letter 'B'.

The average person inherently dislikes work and will avoid it if he can	1 2 3 4 5 6 7 8 9 10	Work is as natural as rest or play
People must be coaxed and made to work	1 2 3 4 5 6 7 8 9 10	People can and do exercise discretion and self-control in their work
People will avoid responsibility if they can	1 2 3 4 5 6 7 8 9 10	People welcome and enjoy real responsibility
Most people do not care about career advancement	1 2 3 4 5 6 7 8 9 10	People are interested in the quality and advancement of their working lives
Most people are basically dull and uncreative for most of the time	1 2 3 4 5 6 7 8 9 10	Most people have great potential, imagination and creativity which is untapped
People see money as the principal real reason for working	1 2 3 4 5 6 7 8 9 10	Money is only one of the benefits of work
People do not want to improve the quality of their own working life	1 2 3 4 5 6 7 8 9 10	People are prepared to put effort into improving the quality of their working life
Objectives are strait-jackets which tie people down	1 2 3 4 5 6 7 8 9 10	Objectives give people incentives and freedom

Activity 8:
Characteristics of personal effectiveness

PURPOSE

Developed and successful individuals the world over display a set of fairly common characteristics. In the same way others continually display a set of characteristics regularly associated with being less successful. This activity is designed to help you see where you stand in relation to the two lists.

HOW TO DO IT

1   On the left side of the characteristics sheet are printed the success characteristics and on the right unsuccessful characteristics. They are deliberately presented as opposites and between the two is a scale. Mark on the scale where you think you are.
2   Check your own perception with the view of others. This can either be done in a dialogue situation or by asking others to rate you using the characteristics sheet.

NOTES AND VARIATIONS

1   An input should be given based on Lecturette 8 'Individual development' or participants should be invited to read it.

Characteristics sheet

I am active	├─┼─┼─┼─┼─╋─┼─┼─┼─┤	I am passive
I seek challenge	├─┼─┼─┼─┼─╋─┼─┼─┼─┤	I avoid challenge
I continually seek self-knowledge and insight	├─┼─┼─┼─┼─╋─┼─┼─┼─┤	I avoid self-knowledge and insight
I use time and energy well	├─┼─┼─┼─┼─┼─╋─┼─┼─┤	I misuse time and energy
I am in touch with my feelings	├─┼─┼─┼─┼─╋─┼─┼─┼─┤	I am out of touch with my true feelings
I continually show concern for others	├─┼─┼─┼─┼─┼─╋─┼─┼─┤	I never show concern for others
I am always relaxed	├─┼─┼─┼─┼─┼─╋─┼─┼─┤	I am always tense
I am always open and honest	├─┼─┼─┼─┼─┼─╋─┼─┼─┤	I tend to manipulate others
I continually try to stretch myself	├─┼─┼─┼─┼─╋─┼─┼─┼─┤	I avoid 'stretching' experiences
I am clear about my personal values	├─┼─┼─┼─┼─╋─┼─┼─┼─┤	I am largely influenced by the views of others
I set high personal standards	├─┼─┼─┼─┼─┼─╋─┼─┼─┤	I set low personal standards
I welcome feedback	├─┼─┼─┼─┼─╋─┼─┼─┼─┤	I avoid feedback
I always see things through	├─┼─┼─┼─┼─┼─╋─┼─┼─┤	I opt out when the going gets tough
I use opposing views	├─┼─┼─┼─┼─┼─╋─┼─┼─┤	I am intolerant to the views of others
I use conflict constructively	├─┼─┼─┼─┼─┼─╋─┼─┼─┤	I avoid conflict
I give freedom to others	├─┼─┼─┼─┼─┼─╋─┼─┼─┤	I try to restrict the freedom of others
I am basically happy with my life	├─┼─┼─┼─┼─┼─╋─┼─┼─┤	I am basically unhappy with my life

Activity 9:
My meetings with others

Almost all of us regularly meet others in our working lives and whether the meetings are formal or informal we can usually make them more useful. This activity helps to assess our present effectiveness and move towards improvement.

HOW TO DO IT

Go through the following steps.
1   Using columns as shown below list those people or groups of people whom you regularly spend time with and how often you meet them in an average week. In the third column rank each meeting in order of importance to you.

People/group I spend time with	Frequency	Importance ranking

2   From the words below (and any others which spring to mind as being appropriate) pick out those which best describe the character of each meeting. Start with the meeting which you ranked highest

in order of importance. Finally, in column three rank each meeting based on the words you have chosen.

Meeting descriptions

formal	unfair	vague	rambling
effective	interesting	superficial	purposeful
great	destructive	messy	friendly
sound	productive	boring	useful
negative	absorbing	irrelevant	stimulating

Ranking effectiveness of meetings

Meeting with	Words chosen	Ranking

3 Compare your ranking in step 1 with that in step 2 and consider which meetings are the ones most in need of improvement.

4 For those meetings you wish to improve complete the work sheet below which will serve as your action plan for change.

Meetings with	Desirable changes in me	Desirable changes in others	What I can do to bring about the changes

NOTES AND VARIATIONS

1   The activity can be adapted to allow completion by a team.
2   It is particularly useful when used in a coaching relationship.

Activity 10:
Use of time

To examine the significance of unimportant and inappropriate activities in our working lives.

HOW TO DO IT

1   List the main activities associated with work with which you are involved during a typical week and write against each the approximate number of hours spent. Remember there are 168 hours in a week and you may regularly spend leisure time considering or progressing work issues. Organise the list with the most time consuming activities at the top. Be as specific as you can. Complete this before going on to the next stage.

2   Now list the activities which you believe are productive or important. Again try to arrange the list with the most significant items at the top.

3   Match the first and second sheets. Consider how far you are spending time on activities which you believe to be unimportant. List separately 'important activities which are not given priority' and 'unimportant activities which require substantial time'. Reflect on your lists for a few minutes. Are there any changes you wish to make?

NOTES AND VARIATIONS

1   The activity can easily be used in a training session or with a group.

2   It can be completed as a total team to assess use of 'team' time and resources.

Activity 11:
Force field analysis

PURPOSE

To provide a framework for a team to systematically tackle a difficult problem.

HOW TO DO IT

1   The activity is carried out individually, and then results are compared in the team.
2   As a team, select a difficult problem that you all feel needs solving. The activity is more useful where other people or groups are also involved in the problem.
3   As individuals work through the following steps.
(a) Identify the problem as you see it now and describe it in writing.
(b) Now define the problem in terms of the present situation and the situation you would like to see when the problem is solved.
(c) Make a list of the forces working against change (resisting forces). Then make a list of the forces working for change (driving forces). These forces can be people, finances, external factors, etc., anything either hindering you from or helping you to make a change.

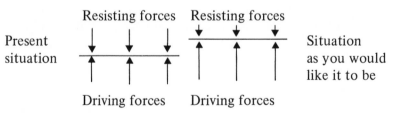

(d) Underline those forces that seem to be the most important.
(e) For each resisting force underlined, list the factors that could possibly reduce or eliminate the force.

(f) For each driving force underlined, list the factors that could possibly increase it.

(g) Determine the most promising steps you could take toward solving your problem and the resources available to help you.

(h) Re-examine your steps and put them in sequence, omitting any that do not seem to fit in with your overall aims. The following column headings may be used as a guide:

Steps When How

4 As a team share the results of individual efforts and formulate a team plan for how you intend to tackle the problem.

NOTES AND VARIATIONS

1 Whilst the activity is written in a format suitable for teams it is also useful to individuals working on individual problems or is also suitable for use in pairs.

2 Activity 12 'Team effectiveness action plan' is an example of how 'Force field analysis' can be used specifically as part of a training event.

Activity 12:
Team effectiveness action plan

PURPOSE

During a training event to enable participants to consider how team effectiveness can be increased 'back home'.

HOW TO DO IT

1   Complete the step by step team effectiveness action plan in the following way:

Steps 1–4 near the beginning of the event;
Step 5 continuously thereafter;
Step 6 near the close of the event.

NOTES AND VARIATIONS

1   This simple activity has been used successfully by the author on many teambuilding events but its introduction must be tailored to the format of the event.
2   A more detailed explanation of 'Force field analysis' (see Activity 11) can be given as an aid to understanding.

TEAM EFFECTIVENESS ACTION PLAN

Step 1: Describe two situations in your organisation which lead you to think that there is a need for teambuilding.

Step 2: Describe two situations where teams are working well together.

Step 3: What forces are working for effective teams?

Step 4:   What forces in your organisation are working against effective teams?

Step 5:   Keep adding to the forces for and against team work as you gain insights during the event.

Step 6:   Prepare an action plan building on positive forces and trying to remove or work round the negative forces.

Activity 13:
Brainstorming

PURPOSE

Many normal operating rules in teams restrict creativity. This activity helps to generate creative ideas and shows how much easier it is to do that when the normal constraints are removed.

HOW TO DO IT

To get the best results, it is important to follow the rules *exactly*.

1   Get together your team and arrange three hours when you can all meet undisturbed.

2   Decide on a subject in which change and creativity are important. If one does not come easily to mind, use the general topic 'ways of improving our teamwork'.

3   Start by explaining that the session is going to try brainstorming, which means that everyone is completely free to suggest ideas. Make it clear that all ideas, no matter how absurd or wild, should be contributed, and that there must be no discussion of an idea; as soon as one is introduced, go on to the next one.

4   Put the rules on a flip chart as a general reminder for the rest of the session.

5   When everyone understands the rules, begin the brainstorming session by writing the chosen topic clearly on the flip chart, for example:

TOPIC
Ways of improving our teamwork

6   Brainstorm this topic for at least forty minutes and list (without judgement or discussion) *every* idea suggested.

7   Now divide the session into two subgroups and ask each group to place each idea into one of these three categories:

A – important and feasible   B – possible   C – worthless

Allow one hour for this phase.

8   Ask each group to list all the 'A' ideas on one sheet, all the 'B' ideas on a second sheet, and all the 'C' ideas on a third sheet.

9   Ask each person to examine both lists of 'A' comments and to choose the two ideas that he feels could make the greatest contribution to improving the business. Each time an idea is chosen put a tick against it.

10   Now take the three ideas with the highest score and ask each subgroup to choose from these the one idea it feels is the most important. Each subgroup is then asked to produce a written plan to carry out the idea.

11   After six weeks, the whole group meets to discuss how well plans are progressing and to take any necessary action.

12   When these first ideas have been successfully implemented, the subgroups can move on to the others. Project teams can also be rearranged.

NOTES AND VARIATIONS

1   This simple technique can be varied to suit almost any situation.

2   It shows how easily ideas come when there is no risk of censorship.

Activity 14:
Team openness exercise

Team effectiveness can be advanced by greater openness amongst team members. This activity helps team members to be more open with each other by exploring work-related topics in greater depth.

HOW TO DO IT

1   Participants should be invited to pair off, preferably with a team member they do not know well.
2   They should then find a comfortable and private place where the following groundrules should be applied:
(a) Take turns asking the questions, choosing them in any order.
(b) Ask only those questions which you are prepared to answer.
(c) Any member may decline to answer any question that is asked of him.
(d) Subsidiary questions may be asked to ensure that replies are fully understood.
(e) Both participants should agree that answers are to remain confidential.
(f) Questions may be asked more than once.

NOTES AND VARIATIONS

1   The activity can also be used in triads or in an open group setting.
2   Similar in concept to Activity 24 'The intimacy exercise' the topics raised are more work-related and less personal.

QUESTIONS TO BE ASKED IN ANY ORDER

1   Are you happy in your present job?
2   Are you effective in your present job?
3   What do you see as the next step in your career development?
4   What personal weaknesses inhibit your performance?
5   What do you regard as your major strengths? What are your main development needs?
6   What are the principal achievements you are looking for in your work right now?
7   Where do you see yourself ten years from now?
8   What do you think that I think of you?
9   What do you think of me?
10   Describe your different responsibilities?
11   What was your first impression of me when first we met?
12   Has your impression of me altered since we first met?
13   How do you respond to pressure?
14   Are you enjoying this activity?
15   What barriers do you see to your own advancement?
16   To whom are you closest in our team?
17   Why do you think that is?
18   How committed are you to our team?
19   What is the major contribution you make to our team?
20   Do you receive sufficient feedback from other team members?
21   Do you think I am devious?
22   Does anything about me puzzle you?
23   Describe the politics of our team to me.
24   How do you think our team is seen by the rest of the organisation?

Before closing the activity each person should answer:

1   How could we better help each other in our work?
2   How else can we jointly improve the effectiveness of our team?

Activity 15:
Review and appraisal meetings

PURPOSE

In any team there needs to be constant concern with 'what has to be done' and 'how best results can be achieved'. A discipline of regular target setting and review often helps team members to work more effectively. In addition, the intention is to give each employee an accurate view of how the company values his contribution and to enable all concerned to understand what has to be done in order to improve performance. Special attention is paid to what the person needs to learn in order to better meet future needs.

HOW TO DO IT

The way in which review and appraisal is tackled can vary. In some larger organisations formal appraisal schemes are introduced which involve a general organisational commitment, a great deal of planning and often an elaborate system of paperwork. Many books and articles have been written about such schemes and anyone wishing to introduce this more formal type of scheme should consult them. To help in this a list of those recommended by the author is included in Part III.

This activity is intended for the manager or team leader who wishes to adopt a more informal approach to review and appraisal and use basic principles in a relatively unstructured way. To do this follow these simple groundrules:

1 Essentially the activity consists of a meeting or series of meetings between two or more people in which they seek to review the past and try to learn from the experience, and so improve the future.

2 You will need to decide such things as:

(a) the interval between reviews;

(b) who is going to be involved in the scheme;

(c) the basis on which the review will be carried out;

(d) whether the scheme is likely to conflict with any other established practices.

3   It is essential to obtain commitment from all those who are to be involved in the scheme and the first thing to do is to explain to everyone what you intend to do.

4   At an early stage you should decide whether you wish to keep any records concerned with appraisal. It is often useful particularly to have the 'areas of achievement' recorded in writing and to use this record as the basis for the next review.

5   One of the weaknesses of many review and appraisal schemes is that they concentrate on personality rather than performance. Personality should only be considered if it is seen to be a barrier to good performance. Therefore, it is necessary to agree with each individual the achievements and standards expected from him or her as a 'datum level' and this agreement should be confirmed at each meeting.

6   It must always be borne in mind that review and appraisal is a two-way process. Always ensure that the individual who is being appraised assesses his own performance against the agreed areas of achievement as well as you doing it yourself. In this way people are more likely to recognise their own weaknesses and development needs and hence be more committed to action. Most people really do appreciate being given feedback on how well or badly they are performing and this part of the scheme can be made more comfortable by asking the individual to relate his own self-assessment first before you make your own comments.

7   Remember that others may also have a legitimate and valuable view about the person's performance. Always ask for other opinions if it will help to produce a more accurate assessment but you should always make it clear to the person being reviewed that you are doing this.

8   Remember that the end product of any review and appraisal approach is action – improvement targets which are agreed and regularly reviewed and development activities which are arranged and followed up.

NOTES AND VARIATIONS

1   This informal approach to review and appraisal offers a manager

or team leader the chance of making a more objective assessment of the individual development needs of his/her team members. It also allows the individual to be involved in the process of identifying his/her own development needs. It need not be a ritual which happens once a year to please the personnel department. It can be varied in timing and method to suit the needs of you and your staff.

2   The approach is particularly useful where:

(a) individuals need a view on their worth to the organisation;

(b) individuals need a clearer understanding of their career prospects within the organisation;

(c) there is low development.

3   More detailed guidance on review and appraisal meetings can be found in the publications mentioned in Part III.

Activity 16:
Enlivening meetings

Often regular meetings become dull and uninteresting and people do not contribute at their optimum level. This activity is designed to increase the involvement of all participants in a regular meeting.

HOW TO DO IT

1 Select a regular meeting which needs to be enlivened.
2 Disregard the usual rules for conducting the meeting; do not prepare a written agenda or have predetermined seating arrangements.
3 List what you want to discuss on a flip chart. Ask others to add to the list. Decide together in what order you will discuss the items.
4 If time is short, decide as a group when you will finish the meeting and, if necessary, put a time limit on each item.
5 Allow ten minutes at the end to answer these questions:
(a) How did today's meeting compare with previous ones?
(b) Have we learned anything that we should do next time?

NOTES AND VARIATIONS

1 This simple technique can enliven even the dullest of formal meetings.
2 Do not forget the learning which is to be applied at the next meeting.

Activity 17:
How good a coach are you?

PURPOSE

To allow those who lead teams to assess their own attitude and practices towards developing others by means of coaching. The activity also gives valuable pointers to the skills and behaviour required of a good coach.

HOW TO DO IT

1 Complete the questionnaire honestly by selecting one answer to each question.
2 Check your score using the score sheet.

NOTE

1 The natural follow-on to this activity is 18: 'Being a better coach'.

How you rate as a coach questionnaire

1   During a typical month do you devote at least two hours of your time to developing each of your staff?
(a) Rarely, if ever.
(b) Occasionally, when things work out that way.
(c) I try hard to and usually succeed.
(d) I always spend more than that amount of time on coaching.

2   Do you:
(a) Plan in advance specific 'coaching assignments' or learning opportunities for your staff?
(b) Keep an eye open for situations which you can use for coaching purposes?
(c) Let your staff learn by the experiences which come their way in the normal course of business?
(d) Consciously create coaching situations – even at the expense of some immediate operational efficiency?

3   Who does most of your work when you are away on leave, or otherwise absent from the office?
(a) Someone always picks up the urgent things; the rest can wait.
(b) Your boss.
(c) Your staff.
(d) Nobody. If the job is to be done properly, only you can do it – so you tackle it when you get back.

4   If the performance of a member of your staff on a particular assignment clearly indicates a weakness in an area where you yourself have special expertise, would your inclination be to:
(a) Tell him exactly what he ought to have done and ensure that someone supervises him closely next time?
(b) Avoid delegating that type of work to him in the future?
(c) Send him on a course?
(d) Get him to tackle another assignment of the same sort, ask him to report progress periodically, and review and discuss his problems as they arise?

5   If a member of your staff comes and asks you what he should do about a problem which has arisen in connection with a task delegated to him, do you:
(a) Tell him to come back in a couple of days, when you have the time to think about it?
(b) Tell him politely that it is *his* job to find the answers, not yours?
(c) Tell him what he should do?
(d) Ask him what *he* would suggest should be done, and how?

Your rating as a coach score sheet

Scoring   Your score

1   a   b   c   d
    1   2   3   4

2   a   b   c   d
    4   2   1   3

3   a   b   c   d
    3   1   4   2

4   a   b   c   d
    3   1   2   4

5   a   b   c   d
    3   2   1   4

                                              Total:

Now read off your rating:

0–10   You really need to work hard at improving your coaching skills.

11–16   You are within reach of being a good coach.

17–20   You should be sharing your skill with others to help them become better coaches.

Adapted from the Food, Drink and Tobacco Industry Board's *Development at Work.*

Activity 18:
Being a better coach

PURPOSE

The team leader has a vital role to play in the development of his team by operating as a coach or counsellor. Many team leaders accept this as sound common sense and have a genuine desire to play their part. For a variety of reasons – time or work pressures, disapproval from others, unwillingness to break new ground – this desire is often not converted into reality. Sometimes team leaders feel they have not got the expertise to master this new 'technique'.

HOW TO DO IT

Consider the following guidelines about coaching.

1 Essentially coaching is the process of *setting tasks, monitoring progress, reviewing and learning from performance*.
Each of these apparently simple steps requires just a little more explanation.

Setting tasks
(a) Each task should have a learning target.
(b) Each task should be appropriate to the learner's ability, experience and development needs.
(c) Each task should be capable of being monitored, e.g. dates, reports, collection of information.

Monitoring progress
(a) Meet regularly to discuss progress.
(b) Try to avoid providing answers (if you know them); let the learner find out for himself. Ask questions such as: 'What do *you* think?' or 'What would *you* propose?'

Reviewing and learning from performance
(a) Review when tasks are complete.
(b) Carry out a thorough post mortem, e.g.
    Why did this work well?
    How could we improve even more?
    What went wrong?
    How could it have been avoided?
    What should we do next time?

2   The skills required are the basic skills of the effective manager.
(a) To be able to listen carefully.
(b) To support the learner at all times.
(c) To help the learner analyse his own shortcomings and strengths.
(d) To set clear and attainable goals/objectives.
(e) To be aware of the feelings and needs of others.

3   Plan to improve your coaching by completing the 'action plan for coaching'.

NOTES AND VARIATIONS

1   A useful lead-in to this activity is 17: 'How do you rate as a coach?'
2   See also the list of publications in Part III.

ACTION PLAN FOR COACHING

Learner's name/job title:

1   Opportunities: What changes do you want to achieve?

2   Targets: How will you know when the change is accomplished?

3   Timing: How long will this take until completion?

4   Tactics: What specific activities/methods will you use?

5   Monitoring: How and when will you monitor progress?

Check the following:
(a) Are the aims of the coaching important to both of you?
(b) Do the proposed methods offer a reasonable chance of success?
(c) Have you adequate resources to carry out the plan?

Adapted from the Food, Drink and Tobacco Industry Training Board's
Development at Work.

Activity 19:
Counselling to increase learning

This activity enables two colleagues to assist each other in defining and tackling their individual development needs.

HOW TO DO IT

Ask a colleague who also wishes to improve his learning/development to help you with this activity and work through the following steps.

1   Each person completes the questionnaire by circling what he thinks is his position on the scale.

2   This step should be completed by both people.

(a) First spend at least ten minutes discussing both sets of answers with the aim of identifying for yourself the *other person's* learning characteristics.

(b) Now complete the profile dealing with the *other person's* learning style.

(c) Following that, list five ways in which the other person can progress and develop his ability to learn.

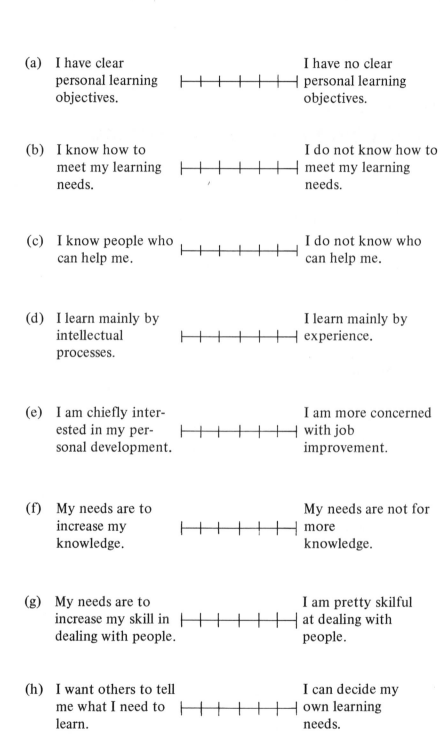

(a) I have clear
     personal learning   ├──┼──┼──┼──┼──┤   I have no clear
     objectives.   personal learning
                                                      objectives.

(b) I know how to
     meet my learning   ├──┼──┼──┼──┼──┤   I do not know how to
     needs.   meet my learning
                                                      needs.

(c) I know people who   ├──┼──┼──┼──┼──┤   I do not know who
     can help me.   can help me.

(d) I learn mainly by
     intellectual   ├──┼──┼──┼──┼──┤   I learn mainly by
     processes.   experience.

(e) I am chiefly inter-
     ested in my per-   ├──┼──┼──┼──┼──┤   I am more concerned
     sonal development.   with job
                                                      improvement.

(f) My needs are to
     increase my   ├──┼──┼──┼──┼──┤   My needs are not for
     knowledge.   more
                                                      knowledge.

(g) My needs are to
     increase my skill in   ├──┼──┼──┼──┼──┤   I am pretty skilful
     dealing with people.   at dealing with
                                                      people.

(h) I want others to tell
     me what I need to   ├──┼──┼──┼──┼──┤   I can decide my
     learn.   own learning
                                                      needs.

THE OTHER PERSON'S LEARNING PROFILE

Comment against the headings below

Clarity of objectives :
Confidence in meeting needs :
Use of help and guidance :
Intellectual/experience learning methods :
Personal/job development :
Knowledge needs :
Skill needs :
Dependence on others :

3   Complete this step either individually or as a pair.
List what you intend to do to actively progress *your own* learning,
using the column headings below as a guide.

Activity	How?	When?

Adapted from the Food, Drink and Tobacco Industry Training Board's
Development at Work.

Activity 20:
Management style

PURPOSE

To enable participants to examine their own beliefs about people against McGregor's Theory X–Y model.
To provide direct feedback of how others perceive a person's management style.
To stimulate general discussion about management style.

HOW TO DO IT

1   Participants are invited to complete the 'My views about people' sheets.
2   The facilitator gives a brief explanation of McGregor's Theory X–Y model (an outline will be found in Lecturette 6 'Appropriate leadership').
3   The facilitator invites participants to score the 'My views about people' sheets in accordance with the key to scoring so that each participant has a total score between 0 and 45. The nearer a score is to 0 the greater the Theory X orientation and the nearer to 45 the greater the Theory Y orientation.
4   The facilitator draws a scale from 0–45 on a large flip chart. He invites each participant to indicate his total score and marks that person's initials on the chart to indicate this (see example scale on page 105).
5   Each participant in turn is given feedback from the others about how far they see his score reflected in his day to day actions.
6   The facilitator leads a discussion based on the 'Discussion topics' sheet.

NOTES AND VARIATIONS

1   This activity is best conducted with a group who normally work together.

2   It is designed to be deliberately direct and confronting and it often produces scenes of great hilarity and amusement as people reveal their individual scores.

3   There are many other similar activities which have been developed around McGregor's X–Y model.

My views about people

The following statements represent views which people commonly hold about other people at work. Consider each pair of statements for a few moments and in each case circle the line on the scale which most accurately represents your view.

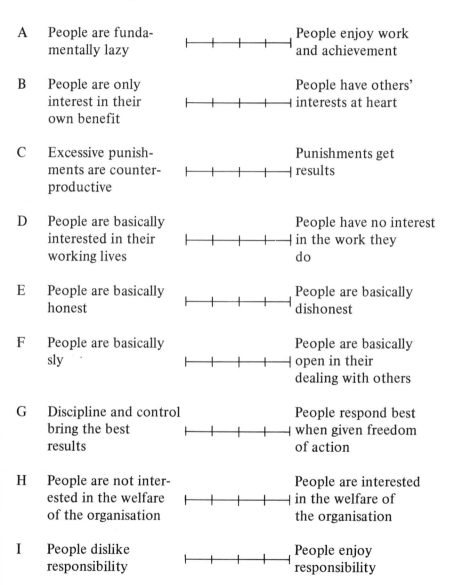

A   People are funda-   People enjoy work
    mentally lazy   and achievement

B   People are only   People have others'
    interest in their   interests at heart
    own benefit

C   Excessive punish-   Punishments get
    ments are counter-   results
    productive

D   People are basically   People have no interest
    interested in their   in the work they
    working lives   do

E   People are basically   People are basically
    honest   dishonest

F   People are basically   People are basically
    sly   open in their
                                                    dealing with others

G   Discipline and control   People respond best
    bring the best   when given freedom
    results   of action

H   People are not inter-   People are interested
    ested in the welfare   in the welfare of
    of the organisation   the organisation

I   People dislike   People enjoy
    responsibility   responsibility

Score sheet

Score each set of statements according to which of the 5 positions on each scale you have marked. Do this as follows:

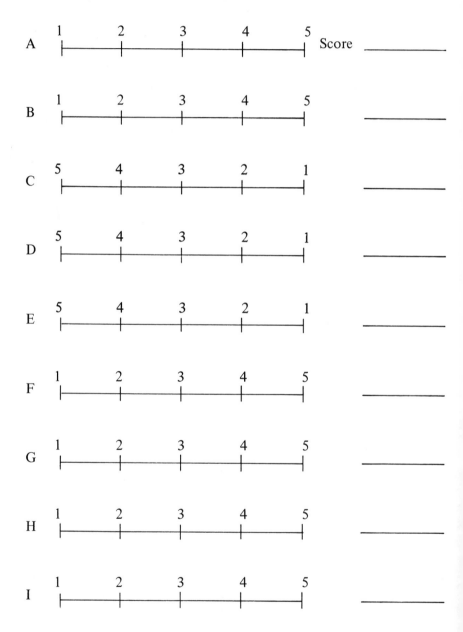

Example scale

Discussion topics

1   How important do we feel style flexibility is?

2   To what extent is it necessary to adapt leadership style when dealing with different groups of workers?

3   How threatening was the activity?

4   To what extent do we agree that a Theory Y leadership style achieves better team results?

5   Is it desirable to aim for an organisational 'Management style'?

Activity 21:
Discussing values

To facilitate discussion of 'value issues' which are commonly found in working teams. Often people are accustomed to discussing facts but less used to discussing issues which involve values, feelings and emotions.

HOW TO DO IT

The facilitator invites groups of between four and eight people to discuss what their attitudes would be if confronted by any of the following situations.

1   You have discovered that a close friend is fiddling the petty cash in another department.

2   You are required by your boss to help conceal from the auditors information which you know could get the organisation into trouble.

3   The organisation has decided on policy about immigrant recruitment which is in conflict to your own deeply held views.

4   You are required to fire a worker for persistent absenteeism but you know that his absence is entirely due to tragic domestic circumstances.

5   You are responsible for consultations with trade union representatives. The organisation has a policy of open and honest communication with trade unions but you honestly believe that this is counter productive.

6   You have lost faith in the organisation and its aims and yet you feel you would be unable to find a job which offered similar financial rewards.

7   You have strong views about the environment and know that the organisation is adding considerably to pollution in order to increase profits.

8   Another manager has confided that he will be leaving in three months. Both he and you know that his promotion is imminent and crucial to the future plans of your own department unless senior management are informed immediately.

NOTE

1   Activity 27 'Cave rescue' is another way of facilitating discussion of value issues.

Activity 22:
Team member development needs

PURPOSE

In the end people must be responsible for their own development. Organisations can create learning opportunities but only individuals can utilise them. If team members are to feel responsibility for, and ownership of, their own development, they need to be involved in establishing their own development needs and they need to take steps to aid their own development. This activity is designed to help individual team members to do this.

HOW TO DO IT

1 Each team member fills out a copy of the development needs sheet.
2 He (she) then discusses it with whoever can be most helpful to him (her). This may be a colleague, friend, wife, husband, a specialist in personal development or the person's boss, etc.

NOTES AND VARIATIONS

1 This activity can easily be allied to appraisal schemes.
2 It can be used to get a 'quick feel' of individual development needs in an organisation or team.
3 Particularly useful where participants need to feel clear ownership of development activity.
4 Results can be pooled to form the basis of a 'unit' or 'team' plan.

Development needs sheet

1   Name:

2   Position in organisation:

3   What are the key activities that you perform? Try to list them in order of importance.

4   Do you anticipate any significant changes in any of these activities during the next year or so?

5   What aspects of your job give you the most problems at present?

6   In what areas do you think you could make a significantly greater contribution to team performance?

7   In what ways do you think you need to develop as an individual? What learning would help you to:
    (a) meet the challenges of the changes listed in (4);

    (b) deal with the problems listed in (5);

    (c) help you make a greater contribution to your team's performance;

(d) aid your development as an individual?

8   Which of these learning methods would be most relevant to you? Indicate order of priority by ranking from 1 to 12, 1 being most relevant.

	1 Management education course at a business school.
	2 Short job-related courses/seminars.
	3 Visits to other companies, etc.
	4 Reading.
	5 Internal courses at present available.
	6 Coaching by your manager.
	7 Coaching by others.
	8 Discussions with colleagues.
	9 Projects/planned experience.
	10 Transfer to another section or function.
	11 Course in human relations management.
	12 Action-based workshop.

9   Make a specific proposal to meet your development needs, establishing your own objectives and preferred method of learning.

10   What resources or which people would you need to help with this proposal?

11   What steps do you need to take to translate the proposal into action?

Activity 23:
Who are you?

PURPOSE

1   To develop relationships as a prelude to working on deeper issues.
2   To practise listening skills.

HOW TO DO IT

1   Ask the group to split into pairs and interview each other in order to find out 'who' the other person is. Participants should try to find out not only about their partner's job and main job concerns, but about their family and cultural life, hobbies, etc. Take twenty minutes for this stage (ten minutes for each interview).
2   After stage one tell participants to report as if they are the other person. One way of helping this is for person A to stand behind person B (who is seated) and speak in the first person singular, using the information obtained in the interview.
3   Lead a discussion on the experience, asking:
(a) How well did you listen?
(b) Would your listening have improved if you had known stage two would follow?
(c) How did it feel to become another person?
(d) How well did your partner do in listening and feeding back?
(e) How well did you do in communicating yourself to him?

NOTES AND VARIATIONS

1   To aid understanding of the process, facilitators can demonstrate stage one.

2   It is important not to introduce stage two before completion of stage one.

3   It is particularly useful as an 'unfreezing' activity at the beginning of a training event and with groups who have not met before.

4   When used as a 'starter' for a training event pairs can also interview each other as to expectations of the event. The facilitator may chart this information during stage two and use it to review progress as the event proceeds.

Activity 24:
Intimacy exercise

Most working relationships exist at a fairly superficial level. This activity is designed to help us get to know others in greater depth. Its specific aims are:
(a) to experience self-disclosure;
(b) to accelerate the getting-acquainted process in teams;
(c) to experience talking about taboo topics;
(d) to develop authenticity between team members.

HOW TO DO IT

1   Approximately one and a half hours is required to complete this activity, together with sufficient space for pairs to talk privately without disrupting each other.
2   The facilitator introduces the exercise with a brief input on self-disclosure and the building of trust which can be taken from Lecturettes 2 and 3. He explains the purpose of the activity.
3   Team members pair off, preferably with people whom they know least well.
4   'Intimacy exercise guidelines' are described, the groundrules are explained, and the forms are then distributed.
5   Pairs meet for approximately one hour following the guidelines and groundrules.
6   Optionally, the facilitator may convene a further meeting of the whole group to discuss the experience.

NOTES AND VARIATIONS

1   Many people feel that the degree of candidness that is required for this activity is undesirable or unacceptable, particularly in a work-

ing environment. It must therefore be an individual choice to participate and facilitators should ensure they do not feel threatened if
they choose to opt out. This exercise can in a short period create
a massive increase in openness between individuals and, if extended,
within and between teams.

2   Where weather and physical conditions allow, and the activity is
being used as part of a team development event, a more conducive
atmosphere can be achieved by inviting participants to leave the
formal training situation and walk around outside whilst talking.

3   Optionally, participants can be invited to form their own additional questions.

INTIMACY EXERCISE GUIDELINES

During the time allotted for this activity you are asked to question your partner from the list overleaf. The questions vary in terms of their intimacy, and you may want to begin with some relatively less intimate ones. Unless you decide otherwise you should take turns at initiating the questions. Follow these groundrules throughout:

1 Your conversations with your partner are to be held in confidence throughout.
2 Any question that you ask your partner you must be willing to answer yourself.
3 You may decline to answer any question initiated by your partner.
4 You may opt out of the activity at any point if you so wish.

INTIMACY EXERCISE QUESTIONS

What is your name?
What is your favourite colour?
Are you or your parents divorced? Have you ever considered divorce?
How much wealth do you have?
How important is money to you?
What attracts you most about members of the opposite sex?
What do you regard as your least attractive features?
What feature of your appearance do you consider most attractive to
    members of the opposite sex?
What turns you off the fastest?
Which major political party or approach do you subscribe to?
Why do you subscribe to that approach?
How do you feel about inter-racial dating and marriage?
What turns you on the most?
What do you regard as the chief defect in your personality?
Do you believe that others have had supernatural experiences?
Have you ever had a supernatural experience?
Have you any health problems? What are they?
Do you think you should have been arrested for anything?
Have you ever been arrested or fined for violating any law?
Have you ever had a mistress?
Have you ever experienced premarital or extramarital sex?
How do you feel about people living together without being married?
What is the most serious lie you have told?
In your early life did you ever lie about a serious matter to either
    parent?
Have you ever cheated on exams?
What do you feel most ashamed of in your past?
Do you subscribe to a private medical scheme?
What is your favourite hobby or leisure interest?
What is the source of your financial income?
How important is religion in your life?
Do you believe in God?
Are you good at sports?
What do you think about the position of females in society?
How could you improve your present domestic situation?
What activities did you most enjoy taking part in at school?
How do you feel about crying in the presence of others?
What were you most punished or criticised for when you were a child?

With what do you feel the greatest need for help and support?
What are your career ambitions?
What is your view about immigration into this country?
How are you feeling about me?
What is the subject of your most frequent fantasy?
What do you think about nudity?
What is the subject of the most serious quarrel you have had?
What makes you sad?
What could you do to improve your life right now?
What is your favourite TV or radio programme?
How intelligent do you think you are?
What was your biggest failure in life?
Is there any feature of your personality that you are proud of? What
   is it?
Do you believe in life after death?
To which person in your life could you respond the most and how?
What are you most reluctant to discuss now?
What foods do you like?
What foods do you dislike?
Do you think women should be allowed to give birth at home?
Is there any person you wish would be attracted to you? Who? (Give
   name)
For whom do you feel the greatest pity?
What emotions do you find it most difficult to control?
What, if any, subjects would you be prepared to take part in a public
   demonstration about?
Have you ever been tempted to kill someone else?
Have you ever been tempted to commit suicide?
What have you needed to see a doctor about in the past year?
Who would you most like to manipulate?
Do you enjoy manipulating or directing people?
Do you smoke marijuana or use any other form of drug?
How many times have you been drunk?
How do you feel about swearing?
Do you drink alcohol in excess?
With whom would you most like to be right now?
What associations do you disapprove of?
To what clubs or associations do you belong?
Who in your team don't you like?
If you could be anyone besides yourself who would you be?
If you could choose a new name what would it be?

Have you ever engaged in homosexual activities?
What is your main complaint about your team?
Do you have any misgivings about members of your team?

Activity 25:
Highway Code – a consensus-seeking activity

PURPOSE

1   To study information-sharing and consensus-seeking activity within a group.
2   To contrast the results of individual and group decision-making.
3   To study the features of effective group working.

HOW TO DO IT

(1)   Any number of groups of 5–8 participants may take part in the activity. Approximately 1½ hours should be allowed.
(2)   The facilitator distributes 'Highway Code' question sheets and individual answer sheets to each participant.
(3)   Up to 15 minutes are allowed in which individual answer sheets are completed. Participants may not discuss questions or answers but should work privately.
(4)   The whole group meets together to complete the group answer sheets. As far as possible the group should discuss the possible answers and reach consensus on group answers. Voting should be avoided. Thirty minutes are allowed for this stage.
(5)   The facilitator distributes the model answer sheets and both individual and group answer sheets are scored.
(6)   A score sheet is distributed to and completed by each group.
(7)   The facilitator leads the group in a discussion of the results of the activity, focusing particularly on the issues listed on the review sheet. At least 30 minutes should be allowed for this stage.

NOTES AND VARIATIONS

1   Process observers can be used and their observations used at the review stage.

2   A number of groups may be directed simultaneously and results contrasted.

3   Facilitators may form their own list of questions from the Highway Code.

Question sheet

1 There are four instances in which overtaking on the left is permissible. What are they?

2 What, according to the Highway Code, are the overall shortest stopping distances on a dry road?
(a)   At 30 mph
(b)   At 70 mph

3 Between what times is the use of a horn prohibited in a built-up area?

4 Name four categories of people or vehicles who are debarred from using motorways.

5 Draw or describe the traffic sign for 'No Overtaking'.

6 Describe the symbol used on vehicles carrying 'Poisonous Substances'.

7 Describe the symbol used to show a level crossing ahead without barrier or gate.

8 How long must a commercial vehicle be before it must display the words 'Long Vehicle' at its rear?

9 What does a single yellow line along the edge of a carriageway denote?

10 What is the sign for 'Hospital Ahead'?

Individual answer sheet

Question	Answer	Score
1(a)		
(b)		
(c)		
(d)		
2(a)		
(b)		
3		
4(a)		
(b)		
(c)		
(d)		
5		
6		
7		
8		
9		
10		

Group answer sheet

Question	Answer	Score
1(a)		
(b)		
(c)		
(d)		
2(a)		
(b)		
3		
4(a)		
(b)		
(c)		
(d)		
5		
6		
7		
8		
9		
10		

Model answer sheet

(Answers are based on the 1978 published Highway Code)

Question 1 (a) When the driver in front has signalled his intention to turn right.
(b) When you intend to turn left at a junction.
(c) When traffic is moving slowly in queues and the lane to your right is moving more slowly than you.
(d) In one-way streets.

Question 2 (a) 75 ft
(b) 315 ft

Question 3 23.30 to 7.00

Question 4 Any four from pedestrians
learner drivers
pedal cycles
motorcycles under 50cc
invalid carriages (some)
agricultural vehicles
horse-drawn vehicles
slow-moving vehicles with oversized loads.

Question 5 A red circle containing a black car at the left-hand side and a red car at the right-hand side.

Question 6 A skull and crossbones and the word 'poison' on dia-mond-shaped background.

Question 7 A railway engine in a red triangle.

Question 8 13 metres.

Question 9 No waiting during every working day.

Question 10 A large white H and the word HOSPITAL on blue square background.

Instructions for scoring

Question   1   Score 1 for each of the 4 correct answers.
Question   2   Score 3 for each of the 2 correct answers.
               Score 1 for each answer which is within 10 per cent of
               the correct answer.
Question   3   Score 1 for a correct answer.
Question   4   Score 1 for each correct answer up to a maximum of 4.
Question   5   Score 1 for a correct answer.
Question   6   Score 1 for a correct answer.
Question   7   Score 1 for a correct answer.
Question   8   Score 2 for a correct answer.
               Score 1 for within 10 per cent of the correct answer.
Question   9   Score 1 for a correct answer.
Question 10   Score 1 for a correct answer.

Score sheet

One sheet should be completed for each group *prior* to review.

1 Group score	
2 Average individual score	
3 Difference between 1 and 2	
4 Best individual score	
5 Difference between 1 and 4	
6 Worst individual score	
7 Difference between 1 and 6	

Review sheet

The following topics should be considered:

1 The difference between the group score and the average individual score.

2 The difference between the group score and the best individual score.

3 The difference between the group score and the worst individual score.

4 The extent to which group resources were utilised in reaching consensus.

5 How leadership was exercised within the group.

6 How well time was utilised.

Activity 26:
Is the team listening?

PURPOSE

'There are those who listen and those who wait to talk.' Many of the activities associated with helping groups to develop require a high level of listening skill. Some people are naturally good at this while others are poor. Some people find it difficult to accept the importance of listening. This activity helps develop this skill in teams. It can prove a rewarding, revealing and, on occasions, amusing activity.

HOW TO DO IT

1 This activity is best attempted as a separate exercise but it can form part of a normal meeting's activities.
2 Divide the participants into small groups of four or five and give them a controversial topic to discuss, for example:
(a) banning dogs from public parks;
(b) the allocation of parking spaces;
(c) merit versus seniority in determining promotion;
(d) women as managers;
(e) compulsory religious education in schools.
It is helpful if you are able to distribute different known points of view in the different groups.
3 Ask for a jointly agreed recommendation from the group. Give them a fairly tight constraint, say, 20–30 minutes.
4 At the end of this time, ask each participant to summarise the point of view of all the other participants on separate sheets of paper.
5 Give each person the sheets relating to his own point of view and ask him to score these (either verbally or in writing) for accuracy and completeness.

6   In open session, discuss the following:
(a) the skills required for listening;
(b) the skills required to reproduce an argument;
(c) the skills needed to advance an unpopular view.
7   If possible, repeat the exercise with another topic to give participants a chance to practise the skills identified.

NOTE AND VARIATION

1   Groups can be invited to generate their own topic for discussion.

Activity 27:
Cave rescue

PURPOSE

To study 'values' in group decision-making.
To practise consensus-seeking behaviour.

HOW TO DO IT

1   Any number of groups comprising 4–7 participants may be directed simultaneously.
2   The facilitator distributes a copy of the cave rescue briefing sheet to each participant together with the volunteer personal details sheet.
3   Five minutes are allowed to assimilate the data and then 45 minutes for discussion.
4   At the end of the period one ranking sheet per group is completed and handed to the facilitator.
5   Each member completes a cave rescue review sheet.
6   The facilitator leads a discussion based on the completed review sheets.

NOTES AND VARIATIONS

1   Additional characters can be created.
2   Process observers may be used to help the discussion at the end of the exercise.
3   Some group members may not wish to take part in the activity for ethical reasons. Participation should be voluntary.

CAVE RESCUE BRIEFING SHEET

Your group is asked to take the role of a research management committee who are funding projects into human behaviour in confined spaces.

You have been called to an emergency meeting as one of the experiments has gone badly wrong.

Six volunteers have been taken into a cave system in a remote part of the country, connected only by a radio link to the research hut by the cave entrance. It was intended that the volunteers would spend four days underground, but they have been trapped by falling rocks and rising water.

The only rescue team available tell you that rescue will be extremely difficult and only one person can be brought out each hour with the equipment at their disposal. It is likely that the rapidly rising water will drown some of the volunteers before rescue can be effected.

The volunteers are aware of the dangers of their plight. They have contacted the research hut using the radio link and said that they are unwilling to take a decision as to the sequence by which they will be rescued. By the terms of the Research Project, the responsibility for making this decision now rests with your committee.

Life saving equipment will arrive in fifty minutes at the cave entrance and you will need to advise the team of the order for rescue by completing the ranking sheet.

The only information you have available is drawn from the project files and is reproduced on the volunteer personal details sheet. You may use any criteria you think fit to help you make a decision.

Volunteer 1: Helen
Helen is 34 years old and a housewife. She has four children aged between 7 months and 8 years. Her hobbies are ice skating and cooking. She lives in a pleasant house in Gloucester, and was born in England. Helen is known to have developed a covert romantic and sexual relationship with another volunteer (Owen).

Volunteer 2: Tozo
Tozo is 19 years old and a sociology student at Keele University. She is the daughter of wealthy Japanese parents who live in Tokyo. Her father is an industrialist who is also a national authority on traditional Japanese mime theatre. Tozo is unmarried but has several high-born suitors as she is outstandingly attractive. She has recently been the subject of a TV documentary on Japanese womanhood and flower arranging.

Volunteer 3: Jobe
Jobe is a man of 41 years and was born in Central Africa. He is a minister of religion whose life work has been devoted to the social and political evolution of African peoples. Jobe is a member of the communist party and has paid several visits to the USSR in recent years. He is married with eleven children whose ages range from 6 years to 19 years. His hobby is playing in a jazz band.

Volunteer 4: Owen
Owen is an unmarried man of 27 years. As a short-commission officer he spent part of his service in Northern Ireland where, as an undercover agent, he broke up an IRA cell and received a special commendation in despatches. Since returning to civilian life he has been unsettled and drinking has become a persistent problem. At present he is a Youth Adventure Leader, devoting much energy to helping young people and leading caving groups. His recreation is preparing and driving stock cars. He lives in Brecon, South Wales.

Volunteer 5: Paul
Paul is a man of 42 who has been divorced for six years. His ex-wife is now happily re-married. He was born in Scotland, but now lives in Richmond, Surrey. Paul works as a medical research scientist at the Hammersmith Hospital and he is recognised as a world authority on the treatment of rabies. He has recently developed a low-cost treatment which could be self-administered. Much of the research data is still in his working notebooks.

Unfortunately, Paul has experienced some emotional difficulties in recent years and has twice been convicted of indecent exposure. The last occasion was 11 months ago.

His hobbies are classical music, opera and sailing.

Volunteer 6: Edward

Edward is a man of 59 years who has lived and worked in Barnsley for most of his life. He is general manager of a factory producing rubber belts for machines. The factory employs 71 persons.

He is prominent in local society, and is a Freemason and a Conservative councillor.

He is married with two children who have their own families and have moved away from Barnsley.

Edward has recently returned from Poland where he was personally responsible for promoting a contract to supply large numbers of industrial belts over a five-year period. This contract, if signed, would mean work for another 25 people.

Edward's hobbies include collecting antique guns and he intends to write a book about Civil War Armaments on his retirement. He is also a strong cricket supporter.

RANKING SHEET

Order of rescue	Name
1	
2	
3	
4	
5	
6	

CAVE RESCUE REVIEW SHEET

1 What were the principal criteria used in ranking the volunteers?

2 How far did the group's criteria line up with your own?

3 How comfortable did you feel about making this kind of decision?

4 What behaviours helped the group in arriving at a decision?

5 What behaviours hindered the group in arriving at a decision?

Activity 28:
Initial review

PURPOSE

This activity is designed to provide information about how team members view the team to which they belong as a prelude to further action.

HOW TO DO IT

The technique is most useful for a team that regularly works together and wishes to begin taking steps to improve its performance. Later on other regular methods of review such as 'Team self-review' or 'Process review' can be used.

1   Ask each person to fill out the initial review questionnaire anonymously. These are collected by or returned to a designated person, who collates the various scores and calculates averages for the situation as team members see it and for the desired situation.

2   When the information is charted and averaged, a meeting is arranged at which the team discusses the implications of the data. At least two hours should be set aside for this meeting.

3   The team then decides what steps need to be taken to improve the way the team works. (Other activities can be used to help with this stage.)

NOTES AND VARIATIONS

1   The questionnaire can also be completed at a meeting of the whole team.

2   'Outsiders' can be asked to complete the questionnaire in order to give an extra viewpoint.

3   In place of 'averaging' scores the group can attempt reaching consensus and this activity can be 'processed' in itself to provide extra learning.

4   As with many activities it can be used as a basis for future action, as an introduction to teambuilding activities or as a constant check on the team's progress.

Initial review questionnaire

On the scales below place a P, representing present, and a D, representing desired, over the number which best represents how you (a) see the team and (b) wish to see the team.

Objectivity

Are we objective in the way we tackle things?

| We are never objective | 1 2 3 4 5 6 7 8 9 10 | We are always objective |

Information

| We never obtain and use the necessary information | 1 2 3 4 5 6 7 8 9 10 | We always obtain and use all necessary information |

Organisation

| Our organisation is never suitable for the tasks we have to perform | 1 2 3 4 5 6 7 8 9 10 | Our organisation is always fully suitable for the tasks we are performing |

Decision-making

| Our decision-making methods are always inappropriate | 1 2 3 4 5 6 7 8 9 10 | We always make decisions in the most appropriate way |

Participation

| Participation is always at its lowest | 1 2 3 4 5 6 7 8 9 10 | Everyone participates fully |

Leadership

| We are never led (managed) in an appropriate way | 1 2 3 4 5 6 7 8 9 10 | Our leadership (management) is highly appropriate |

Openness

| Opinions are never expressed openly | 1 2 3 4 5 6 7 8 9 10 | Opinions are always expressed openly |

Use of time

| We always use time badly | 1 2 3 4 5 6 7 8 9 10 | We always use time well |

Enjoyment

| We never enjoy our work | 1 2 3 4 5 6 7 8 9 10 | We always enjoy our work |

Activity 29:
Prisoners' dilemma

PURPOSE

Often we are more concerned with winning than with achieving the optimum result.

This well-tested activity is designed for the following purposes:

1   To explore the trust between team members and the effects of trust betrayal on team members.

2   To demonstrate the effects of competition between teams.

3   To demonstrate the potential advantages of a collaborative approach to solving problems.

4   To demonstrate the necessity of establishing the purpose of any activity.

HOW TO DO IT

1   Two teams are required of no more than eight members each.

2   There should be enough space for the two teams to meet separately without interrupting or disrupting each other. In the centre of the room two chairs for team representatives are placed facing each other.

3   The facilitator explains that the group is going to experience a simulation of an old technique used in interrogating prisoners. (He carefully avoids discussing the objectives of the exercise.) The questioner separates prisoners suspected of working together and tells one that the other has confessed and that if they both confess they will get off easier. The prisoners' dilemma is that they may confess when they should not and that they may fail to confess when they really should.

4   Two teams are formed, named and seated separately. They are instructed not to communicate with the other team in any way, ver-

bally or non-verbally, except when told to do so by the facilitator.

5   Prisoners' dilemma tally sheets are distributed to all participants. The facilitator explains that there will be ten rounds of choice, with the Red team choosing A or B and the Blue team choosing either X or Y.

AX – Both teams win three points
AY – Red team loses 6 points, Blue team wins 6 points
BX – Red team wins 6 points, Blue team loses 6 points
BY – Both teams lose 3 points

6   Round 1 is begun, with teams having three minutes in each round to make a decision. The facilitator instructs them not to write down their decisions until he signals to do so, to make sure that teams do not make hasty decisions.

7   The choices of the two teams are announced for round 1 and the scoring for that round is agreed upon. Rounds 2 and 3 proceed the same way.

8   Round 4 is announced as a special round, with the points payoff doubled. Teams are instructed to send one representative to the centre to talk before round 4. After three minutes of consultation with each other they return to their teams and round 4 begins. The number of points for the outcome of this round is doubled.

9   Rounds 5–8 proceed as in the first three rounds.

10   Round 9 is announced as a special round, with the points payoff squared. Representatives meet for three minutes, and then the teams meet for five minutes. At the facilitator's signal they mark down their choices, and then the two choices are announced. The number of points awarded to the two teams for this round is squared.

11   Round 10 is handled exactly as round 9. Payoff points are squared.

12   The entire group meets to process the experience. The points total for each team is announced, and the sum of the two outcomes is calculated and compared to the maximum possible outcome (126 points). The facilitator may wish to lead a discussion on the effects of high and low trust on interpersonal relations, on win–lose situations, and on the relative merits of collaboration versus competition.

NOTES AND VARIATIONS

1   Approximately one hour is required for this activity.

2   As the procedure is somewhat complicated it helps to tell participants that it is the facilitator's expectation that participants will not fully understand the process until they have played a couple of rounds.

3   Cash can be collected from teams and used as a prize to heighten competitiveness.

4   After the activity the facilitator can give an input based on Lecturette 4: 'Co-operation and conflict'.

PRISONERS' DILEMMA TALLY SHEET

Payoff
Blue team

		X	Y
		+3	+6
A			
		+3	−6
Red team			
		−6	−3
B			
		+6	−3

Round	Minutes	Choice Red	Choice Blue	Cumulative points Red	Cumulative points Blue
1	3				
2	3				
3	3				
4*	3 (representatives) 3 (teams)				
5	3				
6	3				
7	3				
8	3				
9[†]	3 (representatives) 5 (teams)				
10[†]	3 (representatives) 5 (teams)				

*   Payoff points are doubled for this round
[†] Payoff points are squared for this round

Activity 30:
Human structure

To provide a physical task in which the characteristics of team effectiveness can be observed and demonstrated.
A number of groups can be directed simultaneously.

HOW TO DO IT

1   The facilitator explains the task which is to form a three-dimensional static human structure as high as possible which will exist for two minutes.
2   The time allowed is 15 minutes including planning time.
3   A process observer is appointed for each group who also acts as overall timekeeper.
4   The activity is processed by asking the group to prepare a list of characteristics of effective teams and then review performance against that list.

NOTES AND VARIATIONS

1   There is no requirement for the structure to be freestanding or at ground level. For example, supporting structures may be used or groups may form a structure on top of a hill or on a roof to gain extra height. Only the ask as detailed in 'How to do it' should be divulged before the group undertakes the activity.
2   More than one group may be directed simultaneously and the results of other groups can be used during the process stage.

Activity 31:
The Zin obelisk

PURPOSE

1   To study the process of information sharing in teams.
2   To study leadership, co-operation and conflict issues.

HOW TO DO IT

1   The facilitator distributes the group instruction sheets, one to each member of the team.
2   He divides the information cards *randomly* amongst the team members.
3   The team completes the task.
4   The facilitator leads a review of the experience using the review sheet and, if necessary, the answer and rationale sheet.
5   Approximately 25 minutes is required to complete the activity, with additional time for review.
6   Teams of 5–8 participants may take part.

NOTES AND VARIATIONS

1   Any number of groups may be directed simultaneously.
2   Participants may complete review sheets individually before group process takes place.
3   Extra irrelevant information may be introduced to complicate the task.
4   Process observers may be used.

GROUP INSTRUCTION SHEET

In the ancient city of Atlantis a solid, rectangular obelisk called a Zin was built in honour of the Goddess Tina.

The structure took less than two weeks to complete and your task is to determine on which day of the week it was completed. You may share the information you have on the cards but you may not show your cards to other participants.

Information cards
Cards should be prepared measuring approximately 2″ × 3″, with each separate card containing one of the following pieces of information:

The basic measurement of time in Atlantis is a day.

An Atlantian day is divided into Schlibs and Ponks.

The length of the Zin is 50 feet.

The height of the Zin is 100 feet.

The depth of the Zin is 10 feet.

The Zin is built of stone blocks.

Each block is 1 cubic foot.

Day 1 in the Atlantian week is Aquaday.

Day 2 in the Atlantian week is called Neptiminus.

Day 3 in the Atlantian week is called Sharkday.

Day 4 in the Atlantian week is called Mermaidday.

Day 5 in the Atlantian week is called Daydoldrum.

There are 5 days in an Atlantian week.

The working day has 9 Schlibs.

Each worker takes rest periods during the working day totalling 16 Ponks.

There are 8 Ponks in a Schlib.

Workers each lay 150 blocks per Schlib.

At any time when work is taking place there is a gang of 9 people on site.

One member of each gang has religious duties and does not lay blocks.

No work takes place on Daydoldrum.

What is a Cubitt?

A Cubitt is a cube, all sides of which measure 1 Megalithic Yard.

There are 3½ feet in a Megalithic Yard.

Does work take place on Sunday?

What is a Zin?

Which way up does the Zin stand?

The Zin is made of green blocks.

Green has special religious significance on Mermaidday.

Each gang includes two women.

Work starts on the first day of the Atlantian week.

Only one gang is working on the construction of the Zin.

REVIEW SHEET

1   What actions helped the group accomplish the task?

2   Which actions hindered the group in completing the task?

3   How did leadership emerge in the team?

4   Who participated most?

5   Who participated least?

6   What feelings did you experience as the task progressed?

7   What suggestions would you make to improve team performance?

ANSWER AND RATIONALE SHEET

The answer is Neptiminus.

Rationale

1   The dimensions of the Zin mean that it contains 50,000 cubic feet of material.

2   Blocks are 1 cubic foot each, therefore 50,000 blocks are required.

3   There are 7 working Schlibs in a day.

4   Each worker lays 150 blocks per Schlib, therefore each worker lays 1,050 blocks per day.

5   There are 8 workers per day meaning that 8,400 blocks are laid per working day.

6   The 50,000th block is therefore laid on the sixth working day.

7   As work does not take place on Daydoldrum the sixth working day is Neptiminus.

Activity 32:
Clover leaf

To provide an opportunity for teams to study use of resources and creativity. Any number of teams with a minimum of six players each may take part.

HOW TO DO IT

1   The facilitator marks out this shape on the floor or ground:

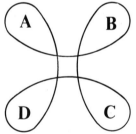

This outline should cover at least 20 feet × 20 feet.

2   He explains that the team is required to produce 'clover leaves' and that the facilitator will purchase these at a set price.

Rules:

(a) A clover leaf is produced each time a person travels completely around the outline.

(b) Each area A, B, C, D must have a person stationed in it at all times.

(c) There must always be an equal number of members in areas A, B, C, D.

3   A facilitator is required to record each clover leaf as it is produced by each team.

4   The activity begins with teams being required to produce the

maximum number of clover leaves in a given time.

5   If two or more teams are used a number of 'rounds' are played to motivate the teams to become more creative in their use of resources and 'production' methods.

6   If only one team is taking part increasingly higher outputs can be required by the facilitator.

7   Planning time of one minute is allowed at the beginning and between each round.

NOTES AND VARIATIONS

1   This activity can be run outdoors quite easily and, as such, provides on a training event a change from more conventional indoor activities.

2   Being 'physical' it provides a good pre-lunch or after lunch activity in an all-day training design.

3   As competitiveness increases or higher outputs are required by the facilitator so creativity of production methods increases.

4   To increase competitiveness further higher prices can be offered for increased production and teams can be placed out of sight of each other.

Activity 33:
Four-letter words

To provide an opportunity for a team to study a range of teamwork issues whilst performing a task which makes increasing demands on them.

HOW TO DO IT

1 A set of 'Scrabble' letters is required which are placed on a table.
2 The facilitator explains that the task is to place as many four-letter words as possible on the table in one minute.
3 Four minutes are allowed for planning and then play commences.
4 Subsequent rounds are played with the facilitator requesting 50, 100, 300 and 1,000 per cent increases in production.

NOTES AND VARIATIONS

1 A number of teams can perform the activity at the same time thus making it competitive.
2 The experience can be processed. Teams often start with an individual approach, then move to a 'division of labour approach' with 'thinkers', 'sorters', 'makers', 'breakers', 'compilers', etc. As increasingly high production requirements are made so less conventional methods tend to be adopted, i.e. just moving two letters about or lifting words up and replacing them in quick succession.

Activity 34:
Team tasks

To provide ideas for simple tasks which a team can complete in a short time and which will provide a basis for reviewing and learning from performance.

HOW TO DO IT

1   The facilitator chooses a task from the list and gives the team time to complete it.
2   Performance is reviewed using one of the activities: (a) 'Process review'; (b) 'Critique'; (c) 'Rating scale for team effectiveness'.

NOTE AND VARIATION

1   Almost any task with which the facilitator is familiar can be used. The activity demonstrates the way in which simple tasks can be utilised as a basis for team learning.

Tasks	Suggested time	Materials required
1 Plan an election campaign to elect one group member to the local council using the resources available to the group.	45 min	Blank posters, pencils, crayons, telephone directory
2 Plan the best way of completing a complicated journey by public transport which involves more than one country and a selection of towns and pre-determined stop over times (facilitator decides on destinations and stop over times).	45 min	Rail, air, sea and road timetables, maps, telephone (optional)
3 Allocate a sum of money to organisation departments or to individuals as a reward for their contribution.	30 min	None
4 Devise a new game to be played with (a) a round ball, (b) 12 sticks, (c) 24 marbles.	30 min	None
5 Design and play a piece of music using oral sounds only and accommodating as many instruments as possible.	15 min	None
6 Decide where to unload 10 cubic metres of tarmacadam to best use before it sets given that it should be laid approximately 2″ thick.	10 min	None
7 Act out a well-known pantomime or fairy story using team members to best advantage.	1 hour	Anything to hand

Activity 35:
Making meetings more constructive

PURPOSE

Meetings are probably regarded as the major curse of modern organisational life. It is not that meetings are a bad thing, it is just that so many are badly used. This activity aims to show that they can be improved and made more constructive if the following features are present:
(a) clear purpose and objectives;
(b) maximum involvement of all participants;
(c) clear and agreed procedures;
(d) review of 'what is going on in the meeting' (the process) at regular intervals.

HOW TO DO IT

1   The first stage should be to decide on the *purpose and objectives of the meeting*. Sometimes these will appear obvious; sometimes they *will be* obvious. In any event, it is advisable to check that all participants are clear. Ideally, all participants should also agree with the purpose and objectives but this will not always be possible. Once clarity has been achieved it is useful to display the purpose and objectives on a chart to concentrate participants' attention when they are inclined to wander.
2   How to achieve the purpose and objectives is the next problem. All participants should have a chance to give their views. From this should emerge:
(a) the agenda;
(b) the decision-making process;
(c) the method of leadership to be employed;
(d) the time allocation for each item.

In some cases, these matters will have been decided in advance but for the sake of involvement and commitment it is valuable to clarify them with all members at the beginning of the meeting.

3 There are a number of ways of *involving participants* in meetings such as:

(a) The use of open-ended questions, e.g. 'What do you suggest?', 'How would you tackle this problem?' These may be addressed either generally or to specific individuals.

(b) Breaking for 10–15 minutes into pairs or threes to discuss a particular item on the agenda.

(c) Rotating the chairmanship.

(d) Asking someone to prepare part of the meeting in advance and giving him/her the opportunity to run that part of the meeting.

(e) Asking someone who has not contributed much to summarise the discussion at various stages.

NOTES AND VARIATIONS

1 The activity can be extended by including 'Process review' or 'Team self-review'.

2 Consider using also 'Enlivening meetings', 'Brainstorming', and 'Is the team listening?'

Activity 36:
Positive and negative feedback

Personal feedback is a feature of many teambuilding events and activities. Often the negative feedback can appear as extremely threatening and can lead to feelings of insecurity. This can be lessened by ensuring that it is accompanied by positive feedback which enhances a feeling of well-being and security. This activity is designed to facilitate both negative and positive feedback simultaneously.

HOW TO DO IT

1   The activity should only be used with a group of people who have had some experience of working together, such as at the conclusion of a series of teambuilding activities or at the end of team development workshop.
2   Sufficient personal feedback sheets are distributed to enable each participant to have one for each other member of the group.
3   Sheets are completed and participants are invited to sign them, but also given the option of leaving them unsigned.
4   Completed sheets are delivered to a central mail box and collated so that each participant can collect all sheets intended for himself.
5   After the messages have been considered participants are asked to:
(a) raise any points of clarification with the entire group;
(b) tell the group about the feedback which has been most helpful to them.

NOTES AND VARIATIONS

1   The activity can be terminated at stage 4.

2 Messages can be shared in pairs, or in the group, or not at all.

3 This activity is particularly useful:

(a) to generate feelings of warmth after a particularly threatening activity or one which involved negative feedback;

(b) at the end of a training event when everyone can depart with a 'personal message' from other participants to take away with him.

4 The activity can also be used to give feedback to the facilitators about an event.

PERSONAL FEEDBACK SHEET

To:

The things I have found most valuable about you are:

Your major strengths are:

Your most helpful actions in this group have been:

Your principal weaknesses in the group are:

The types of behaviour you should try to change are:

From:

Activity 37:
Improving one-to-one relationships

PURPOSE

Sometimes two people who need to work together seem to be constantly at loggerheads. We may feel inclined to knock their heads together. This sometimes works but it is not a development technique which can always be recommended as often the result is nothing better than severe headaches! This activity aims to bring about improvement by:
(a) specifying what each expects of the other;
(b) clarifying where those expectations are not being met;
(c) clarifying how the two can be more helpful to each other.

HOW TO DO IT

1 Ask the two people concerned to make up three lists.
(a) The things valued in the way they have worked together.
(b) The things disliked about the way they have worked together.
(c) The things each thinks will be on the other's lists.
2 A meeting is arranged between the two at which the lists prepared by both are considered as follows: both present list (a), both present list (b), and lastly both present list (c).
It is helpful if a facilitator can be at the meeting.
3 At each stage the facilitator discourages any talk not specifically directed towards gaining an understanding of the other's point of view.
4 Each person then outlines any changes which will help to improve the relationship, and how they could work together to bring these changes about.

5   A list should also be drawn up of the items which the two failed to agree on. Each is then asked to decide how these should be dealt with or whether they should be left for the time being.
6   Remember to follow up these arrangements to ensure they are being carried out.

NOTE AND VARIATION

1   A facilitator is not essential.

Activity 38:
To see ourselves as others see us

To experience and demonstrate openness as a feature of a teambuilding event. To generate further data for use at the event.

HOW TO DO IT

1 Form syndicates, representing as far as possible groups who have been working together on the event.
2 Each syndicate goes to a separate room and takes 20 minutes to prepare on flip charts
(a) a list of adjectives describing each other syndicate;
(b) a list of adjectives describing themselves.
Two rules should be followed: a maximum of 12 adjectives per list is allowed and the group is responsible for the method of preparing the list.
3 Each syndicate distributes to the other syndicates its list of adjectives describing them. It then displays the flip charts it has received together with the one it has prepared about itself.
4 After considering the lists for a few minutes in silence the syndicate spends 20 minutes processing the experience, focusing particularly on:
(a) the difference between the lists of the other syndicates;
(b) the difference between their own and other syndicate lists;
(c) the range of 'positive' and 'negative' adjectives;
(d) whether the syndicate has received any feedback on which it wishes to work during the event.
5 Optionally syndicates may then view each other's lists and the facilitator may lead a plenary discussion on the experience.

NOTES AND VARIATIONS

1   This activity will bring to the surface the feelings of one syndicate for another and the data can be potentially damaging. Therefore, only use the activity if:
(a) syndicates are 'strong' enough to take the data and likely to see it as helpful, or
(b) there will subsequently be time on the event to work through some of the issues raised.
2   With the above reservations this activity can be used to quickly bring inter-team issues into the open where they can be dealt with.
3   Lecturettes 2 and 3 are particularly helpful in highlighting learning from this activity.

Activity 39:
Process review

Process review is one way of studying meetings or activities for the purpose of improving teamwork. Effective teams become effective by looking at the way they function and by learning from the experience.

HOW TO DO IT

1   The activity can be used either with an important meeting you attend regularly or with another activity from the guide. Many are suitable for this kind of review. Appoint one member to become an observer; he will sit outside the team and quietly observe what is happening.
2   The facilitator or the observer himself explains his role which is to watch what happens and at the end of the session report back to the group so that they can all think about their behaviour. This should tell the team and its individual members something about themselves and how they behave as a team and will help the team to modify the way in which it operates in the future.

During the sessions, the observer should look particularly for the following points:
(a) Does everyone understand the purpose of the group?
(b) Is good use being made of the time available?
(c) Are personal aims conflicting with the group's aims?
(d) Is the group avoiding issues that may be difficult or unpleasant?
(e) Do people really listen to others?
(f) Does discussion deal with facts and verifiable information, or does it deal with speculation and opinion?
He should remember that being an observer does not give him any

more abilities or power than other members and that he may observe incorrectly, particularly if it is the first time he has taken part in the activity.

3   The observer takes no part in the discussions but watches carefully what happens.

4   The observer's review at the end of the meeting takes approximately half an hour. Initially, he should use the process review checklist as a guide. He should try to be as helpful as possible by describing, rather than interpreting, what he actually saw.

NOTES AND VARIATIONS

1   More than one observer can be used if required. Where activities are used which require a set number of participants a variation in the number of process observers can ensure that all are employed in useful activity.

2   Where more than one observer is used they should briefly meet together and share observations before reporting back to the whole group.

3   An input based on Lecturette 7 'Regular review' can be given by the facilitator.

PROCESS REVIEW CHECKLIST

Who had the most 'air time'?

Who had the least 'air time'?

How clear was the purpose of the task? Were people committed to it?

How well did people listen to each other?

Were creative ideas suggested?

What happened to creative ideas?

Did the meeting serve to resolve differences?

What actions helped the team most?

What actions hindered the team?

How well was time used?

Were difficult or unpleasant issues raised and resolved?

Did the team deal in facts wherever possible?

Did individual aims conflict?

Activity 40:
How we make decisions

This activity is designed to help participants determine their predominant decision-making style by receiving feedback from other people, and to help a team to establish the decision-making style most frequently used.

HOW TO DO IT

1   The facilitator delivers an input based on the four approaches to decision-making outlined in Lecturette 5 'Sound procedures'.
2   Decision-making styles sheets are distributed to participants.
3   Each team member completes a decision-making styles sheet for the person being reviewed.
4   The scores for each style are calculated and then discussed by the team.

NOTE AND VARIATION

1   Feedback can be given to the person whose style is being reviewed by simply handing him completed forms. This makes the activity less confronting and more comfortable.

DECISION-MAKING STYLES SHEET

Write the name of the person being assessed in the space provided. Each participant has 10 points, all of which are to be used. Allocate your 10 points to one or more of the four styles so that the predominant style receives the highest number of points, and so on. Untypical styles receive no points.

Name:

1   We take the decisions.   ☐ points

2   He makes the decisions himself.   ☐ points

3   He seeks other opinions before he decides.   ☐ points

4   He takes decisions, with people of his choice.   ☐ points

Activity 41:
Team self-review

PURPOSE

To help team effectiveness by reviewing performance. Whilst process review involves the use of an 'outsider' internal review can be conducted without such help.

HOW TO DO IT

All members of a team take part either during or after the completion of a task or meeting.

1   The facilitator explains that 'internal' review is a way of improving team functioning and that if it is to work it demands openness, honesty and a certain amount of risk-taking.

2   Each participant completes a 'Team self-review sheet' in which he rates team performance against the following headings:

Objectivity	Leadership
Information	Openness
Organisation	Support
Decision-making	Use of time
Participation	Climate

3   The team tries as far as possible to reach consensus in completing a further review sheet which reflects the view of the team.

4   The process can be repeated after further meetings or tasks. In many developed teams regular review becomes a way of life.

NOTES AND VARIATIONS

1   The activity is most useful when used repeatedly.

2   The team can consider the appropriateness of the questions and if desired make changes.

TEAM SELF-REVIEW SHEET

Circle those numbers which best indicate your view of how the group performed.

1   Objectivity: How clear were we about the purpose and objectives of the task?

    1   2   3   4   5   6   7   8   9   10
    Unclear   Clear

2   Information: How was the necessary information obtained and used?

    1   2   3   4   5   6   7   8   9   10
    Badly   Very well

3   Organisation: Was our organisation suitable for the task?

    1   2   3   4   5   6   7   8   9   10
    Unsuitable   Suitable

4   Were our decision-making techniques appropriate?

    1   2   3   4   5   6   7   8   9   10
    Inappropriate   Appropriate

5   Did everyone participate fully?

    1   2   3   4   5   6   7   8   9   10
    Low involvement   High involvement

6   Was leadership exercised appropriately?

    1   2   3   4   5   6   7   8   9   10
    Inappropriately   Appropriately

7   Were feelings and opinions expressed openly?

    1   2   3   4   5   6   7   8   9   10
    Not open   Very open

8   Was time used well?

    1   2   3   4   5   6   7   8   9   10
    Badly   Well

9   To what extent did you enjoy working in the group?

    1   2   3   4   5   6   7   8   9   10
    Not at all   Very much

Activity 42:
Silent shapes

PURPOSE

To study problem solving techniques within a team in order to apply
the learning in a work situation.

HOW TO DO IT

1   First make a set of shapes. They can be made with semi-stiff card
and are formed from four squares divided as shown below.

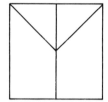 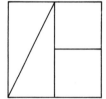 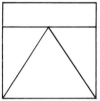 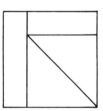

2   All pieces are randomly mixed and put into four envelopes each
containing four pieces.

3   Teams of four people are formed and each person is given one
envelope and the following instructions:

(a)   The team's task is to form four squares from the pieces of card
you all have.

(b)   During the activity you may not speak.

(c)   Cards may be displayed on the table.

(d)   You may not ask for a card from any other team member or
signal your requirement in any way.

(e)   You may give and receive cards only.

4   After the activity a discussion is led by the facilitator using the following key questions:
(a) What did we learn about leadership?
(b) What did we learn about our achievement of the task?
(c) What did it feel like to not be able to communicate the things you wanted to communicate?
(d) What could have helped achievement of the objective?
(e) What learning can we apply in the 'real-work' situation?

NOTES AND VARIATIONS

1   It is usually necessary for the facilitator to 'police' the activity ensuring that rules are strictly adhered to.
2   Two or more groups can be directed simultaneously.
3   Process observers can be used.

Activity 43:
The working clock

PURPOSE

To help individuals make better decisions about the use of time.

HOW TO DO IT

1   Participants are asked to identify the ten major activities in which they are normally involved and to apportion their normal working week between them.

2   A circle is used to represent a 'clock face' of the working week. Individuals are asked to divide the clock face according to the apportionment arrived at in the first stage of the process, as shown below.

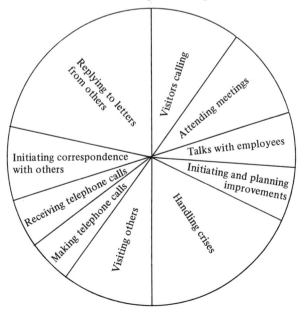

3   Pairs are formed who share diagrams and identify principal differences.

4   With the help of his partner each individual examines his clock face asking questions such as:

(a) To what extent am I reacting rather than initiating?

(b) Do others determine too much of the content of my working life?

(c) Is too much time spent on handling crises?

(d) Do I participate in too many meetings?

(e) Does 'personal development' figure largely enough?

(f) To what extent could my activities be performed by some other person?

(g) Is there a significantly different pattern on different days?

(h) Are physical arrangements conducive to the best use of time (location of secretary, record storage, nearness to processes being managed)?

(i) On whom or what am I spending too much time?

(j) On whom or what am I spending too little time?

(k) What changes should I make in my use of time?

Activity 44:
Basic meeting arrangements

PURPOSE

Often regular meetings follow a set format which inhibits contribution and effectiveness. This activity is designed to highlight which of the 'basics' of meetings need improvement. The activity deals with the 'basics' of meetings rather than interpersonal issues.

HOW TO DO IT

1   Regular attenders at a meeting are invited to complete the 'our meeting review sheet' by awarding marks out of ten for each statement according to their satisfaction.

Thus   0 = I am completely dissatisfied.
        10 = I am completely satisfied.

2   Sheets are collated and presented to the meeting. Items for highlighting can include:
(a)   the area of highest dissatisfaction;
(b)   the area of highest satisfaction;
(c)   total scores for each area;
(d)   total scores for each individual, etc.
3   The team discusses which areas it wishes to improve and decides how it will change arrangements to achieve a greater degree of satisfaction.

NOTE AND VARIATION

1   The process can be repeated to check whether new arrangements have been effected.

OUR MEETING REVIEW SHEET

		Marks out of 10
1	Do we meet at the right frequency?	
2	Are our meetings of the right length?	
3	Are our meetings at the right time?	
4	Do the right people attend?	
5	Are our agendas appropriate?	
6	Do we have the necessary information?	
7	Do we have effective decision-making procedures?	
8	Do we make the right use of external help?	
9	Is our meeting room adequate?	
10	Is it laid out in the right way?	
11	Do we use appropriate aids?	
12	Do we record appropriately?	
13	Do we review our performance?	
14	Do we learn from our mistakes?	
15	Is our policy on chairmanship appropriate?	
16	Is timekeeping satisfactory?	
17	Are refreshment arrangements adequate?	
18	Are potential interruptions handled correctly?	
19	Are our meetings necessary?	
20	Are our meetings useful?	
	Total	

Activity 45:
Decision-taking

PURPOSE

To enable a team leader to examine how his team members perceive decisions to be taken, and to contrast this with how they would wish decisions to be taken.

HOW TO DO IT

1   The team leader introduces the activity with a brief outline of the four decision-making approaches outlined in Lecturette 5.

    1: 'I make the decisions'
    2: 'I seek opinions'
    3: 'I take decisions with people of my choice'
    4: 'The team decides'

2   Participants draw two rectangles which represent decisions taken. They then apportion the first according to: 'How we take decisions' and the second according to: 'How I would prefer us to make decisions' (see example on next page).
3   The team leader considers the completed rectangles and initiates a discussion with the team on steps which can be taken to achieve a greater match.

NOTES AND VARIATIONS

1   Anonymity is usually best if the activity is to be conducted by the team leader.
2   An outside facilitator should always obtain the team leader's consent to the use of the activity.
3   Teams can be contrasted using the activity.
4   The team leader's perceptions can be compared with the average apportionment of the team.

EXAMPLE

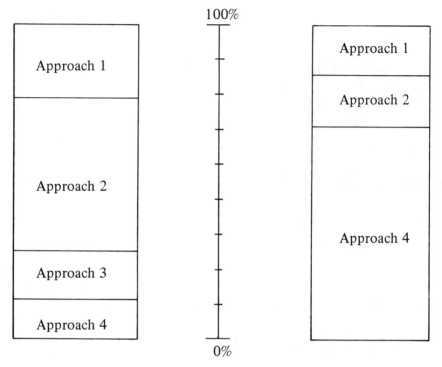

How we take decisions   How we should take decisions

Lecturettes

In writing these lecturettes I have had in mind the following uses.

1   To explain further the 'building blocks' of effective teamwork described in Part I.
2   As notes which the manager/trainer can use to give 'inputs' on training/educational events.
3   To help explain and discuss the outcomes of the activities, particularly when they are used in 'workshop' situations.
4   As theoretical reading for those who wish to understand some of the concepts of team development.
5   As 'hand-out' material before or after training sessions.
6   As follow-up reading or discussion material after using the building blocks questionnaire.
7   To help explain the implications of teambuilding to senior management.

There is one lecturette for each of the 'building blocks':

Clear objectives and agreed goals

Openness and confrontation

Support and trust

Co-operation and conflict

Sound procedures

Appropriate leadership

Regular review

Individual development

Sound inter-group relations

Lecturette 1:
Clear objectives and agreed goals

No group of people is likely to be effective unless it knows what it wants to achieve. As a West Country friend often remarks 'People need to know where they be to'. The first step in achievement is usually realising what it is we want to achieve; usually an intelligent group of people is capable of devising its own methods providing the members are clear on the desired outcome. But having clear objectives and agreed goals is more than just knowing what the outcomes need to be. People are only likely to be committed to objectives if they also feel some identity with and ownership for them, in other words if objectives and goals are discussed and agreed by team members. Often this agreement is difficult to achieve but experience tells us that it is an essential prerequisite of the effective team and that hence it is worth a great deal of trouble to get it right.

All organisations and teams exist for a purpose and yet so often the way in which they operate demonstrates that the purpose is un-clear. If a team has no clear view of what it wants to achieve, then it necessarily follows that individuals cannot contribute in any opti-mum way towards its success. Even where team objectives are under-stood and agreed there is still often a gap between team and personal objectives. One of the chief indicators of effective team working is that this gap has been narrowed as much as possible. This means that effective teams must recognise both personal and group needs. The need for fulfilment, recognition and achievement, for instance, may be very strong in individuals and some people may be quite unhappy in a team unless these individual needs are being met. The effective team allows each individual member to give of his best and to take from the team those things which he needs. Trying to make people the same will not bring about effectiveness.

Some of the main barriers to achieving clear objectives and agreed goals are:

1   The tendency for performance to be judged by input rather than output. In other words, we often measure a man by the way he acts and the things he does rather than the results he achieves at the end of the day. In organisations the world over, people are judged by how smart their dress is, whether they arrive at work on time, whether their desk is tidy, whether they make quick decisions, whether they are polite, and even sex appeal comes into the picture. In job descriptions we find phrases such as 'To organise', 'To report', 'To co-ordinate', 'To administer', rather than phrases which describe the results which are required. This is one of the principal reasons why job descriptions often become straitjackets.

2   Managers and subordinates not sharing a clear understanding of what is expected. This leads to wrong assumptions about the subordinate's ability and means that he is being judged by different standards to those he applies to himself. This problem has been the stumbling block of many so-called performance appraisal schemes.

3   Too often we consider how to achieve a task without really considering whether we should be performing that task at all. One simple test is to confront every task with the word 'why' and to keep asking that question until a satisfactory result is obtained. Only when the question 'why' has been satisfactorily answered should the question 'how' be asked.

Often the system used for monitoring results is inappropriate. One of the best examples I know was that of a team of Government sponsored consultants. They had difficult assignments which demanded considerable initiative, flair and experimentation, and yet they were judged on such things as the number of hours worked and correct completion of administrative forms. No serious attempt was ever made to assess their effectiveness from the clients' viewpoint and, in time, some of them began to see the completion of forms as more important than their clients' needs. 'The system must suit the needs of the business' *not* 'the business must suit the needs of the system'.

Often people confuse 'winning' with achieving objectives. Most people, if they see themselves in a competitive situation, exhibit a desire to win and sometimes this can be quite counter-productive. People are rarely motivated by being beaten.

In order to overcome some of these problems, organisations have introduced elaborate systems and given them names like strategic planning, corporate planning, performance review, and appraisal. Perhaps the most widely used and known is management by objectives and the basis of this is joint agreement on the results which can reasonably be expected, the time it should take and the methods to be used for assessing results. Experience has shown that such formal schemes are of most benefit where people have to work on their own initiative or without close support or in isolated locations. They are less beneficial where people have regular contact with colleagues, work under close supervision or have largely repetitive jobs.

Here are a few golden rules about setting objectives.

1 If objectives are to provide a useful aid to motivation then they need to be democratically conceived.

2 Managers, teams and individuals need to be involved in determining their own areas of responsibility and their own objectives.

3 The emphasis should be on 'results to be achieved' rather than 'things to do'.

4 Managers and subordinates must agree on results required, methods of measuring them, and a timetable for review.

5 The changing environment must be kept in mind throughout.

6 Objectives should as far as possible be (a) specific, (b) time bounded, (c) measurable.

Greater motivation, less demands on management, less conflict, greater creativity, and initiative, less need for punishments and threats, and better use of time and energy are just some of the advantages which come from clear objectives and agreed goals.

One final point to remember is that organisational as well as team and individual objectives need to change. There are countless examples of organisations who may have been clear about objectives in the beginning, but have paid the price of not reviewing them with the passing years. The organisation which looks ahead, foresees difficulties, seizes opportunities and learns to redefine its aims in the light of changing circumstances is the one that ultimately succeeds.

Lecturette 2:
Openness and confrontation

If a team is to be effective then the members of it need to be able to state their views, their differences of opinion, interests and problems without fear of ridicule or retaliation. No teams work really effectively if there is a 'cut-your-throat' or 'stabbing-in-the-back' atmosphere. Where members become less willing or able to express themselves openly much energy, effort and creativity are lost. Similarly there is a need to confront problems and issues rather than avoid them. Effective teams do not avoid delicate or unpleasant issues, they confront them honestly and squarely.

Thus two of the hallmarks of good teamwork are openness and confrontation. They are the attributes which often separate objective, sound teamwork from the shallow charade which passes for teamwork. In many organisations because openness and confrontation are manifestations of both attitude and behaviour, they are slow to appear and difficult to teach, and in most cases are a result of long and diligent teambuilding activities. What we do know is that openness and confrontation improve as the following circumstances come about.

IMPROVEMENT IN COMMUNICATION AND FEEDBACK

As communication between members of a team improves, so openness and confrontation develop. Real communication is candid and honest, and is concerned with genuine understanding and sharing of feelings and experiences. The type of communication which tells others only part of the truth inhibits openness and does not advance teamwork. Crucial to this is the feedback we give to and receive from others. Feedback is generally most helpful where:

(a)   it takes into account the needs of the receiver (and the giver) at that point in time;

(b)   it concentrates on describing events or feelings rather than evaluating them;

(c)   it concentrates on things which the receiver can do something about;

(d)   it is as specific as possible;

(e)   it is timed to be near to the event and at a time when the receiver is receptive to it;

(f)   understanding of it is checked.

INCREASE IN SELF-KNOWLEDGE

As individuals, through teambuilding activities, begin to know themselves better, to know their colleagues better, and to build one-to-one and one-to-all relationships, they find that openness and confrontation also develop. Honest self-knowledge recognises true weaknesses and strengths and admits them to others, so that help can be offered and obtained. Requesting and obtaining help increases mutual understanding and respect amongst team members and fosters genuine openness.

CONSTRUCTIVE USE OF CONFLICT

Conflict, properly managed and constructively employed, leads to greater understanding amongst members of a team. Positive conflict, which deals in facts and is intended to help individuals or the team to improve by talking through problems until sound understanding is reached, encourages both openness and trust. Negative conflict, which relies on rumour and opinion, and is intended to wound and divide, breeds mistrust and hostility.

INCREASE IN ACTIVE LISTENING

Although listening is an aspect of good communication it needs emphasis. In good teams, listening involves more than merely hearing words. It demands a willingness to meet others half-way, and to forget personal feelings while considering others' views. Above all it demands a definite desire to understand the attitude and feelings of the speaker and what he is really trying to say. Active listening can increase when we can:

(a) stop evaluating what we hear as we hear it;
(b) start putting to the back of our minds what we want to say in favour of the speaker;
(c) start 'parking' other things which are on our minds;
(d) stop looking around or being distracted;
(e) stop filtering the information so that we hear what we want to hear.

Openness and confrontation amongst team members also encourages greater creativity. They are not soft options, nor are they superficial values, although they are easily simulated for a short time.

Lecturette 3:
Support and trust

Support and trust naturally go together for without one the other cannot exist. Both can best be achieved where individual team members do not feel they have to protect their territory or function, and feel able to talk straight to other team members about both nice and nasty things. With trust people can talk freely about their fears and problems and receive from others the help which they need to be more effective.

One definition of support is 'to strengthen by assistance'. It is an essential ingredient of an effective team. Support is often confused with sympathy, but the idea that support strengthens means the two are very different expressions of emotion. The sympathetic offering of a shoulder to weep or shower complaints on is not necessarily supportive, and in fact can have a weakening effect on relationships.

People, whether in a family or a firm will never be able to feel frank and open unless they also feel that other members are equally frank and open. Conflict avoided in the name of support is like building relationships on sand. It is also important that people working or living together sense that their shortcomings or mistakes will be accepted along with their strengths and weaknesses, if a healthy, supportive climate is to exist.

Business life involves people in many complex relationships with others. The simple diagram below gives just a small picture of the possible and actual relationships in an organisation:

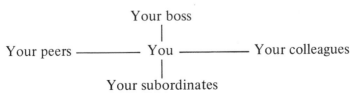

For all of these relationships to be supportive, self and group perceptions need to be clear. One of the problems in achieving support

is often that people's differing backgrounds, values and expectations colour perceptions to such an extent that communication is not reached and support is not possible.

A second factor inhibiting support is competition over 'territory'. People often feel very possessive and defensive over their areas of responsibility, even about the information they have. Access to information can mean power and a developing subordinate can often be seen by an unsupportive boss as a territorial threat.

A third inhibiting factor is the imposition of, rather than the agreement of, goals and performance standards. Support between two people has to be two-way and must be built on a relationship of trust and mutual confidence. It is all too easy for this to be broken by actions or attitudes perceived as domineering, patronising or condescending, and people often feel undermined when they are given targets which have been set with little or no reference to them.

Perhaps the biggest single barrier to support is a low level of trust. Trust takes a long time to achieve but it can be destroyed in a few seconds. You cannot order others to trust you; it only comes through their experience of you and it is perhaps the most difficult thing of all to give through training.

When these inhibiting factors have been overcome, it is possible to create a supportive climate in which people can begin to move towards agreed objectives and support each other with constructive criticism, mutual confidence and frank, direct communications. When people in a team really trust each other true support can be experienced, support which strengthens not confirms weakness.

Lecturette 4:
Co-operation and conflict

Co-operation means working together or, as defined by one dictionary 'working together to share the profits'. Perhaps this is the essence of teamwork – that people put the team's objectives before their own and share both the financial and psychological rewards of their efforts. Co-operation implies that individuals are committed and willing to be involved in the work they do, and that they are ready to share their skills and information with the rest of the team, knowing that the others will reciprocate. People trust each other and encourage others to use their ideas. Everyone in the team is open about their strengths and weaknesses, knowing that they are accepted. This in itself places a great responsibility on the team to foster and maintain the spirit of co-operation and one finds that the members of the team remind and help individuals who may be falling behind with some task.

Co-operation implies that individuals trust other members' ability to consider their interests equally with their own and are willing for people to undertake assignments that contribute to the group's objectives. People are less suspicious of individuals' motives in carrying out important assignments.

Without trust and openness co-operation cannot occur. It is essential that people are able to talk frankly and without fear of looking foolish. The group leader and members need to work hard at achieving co-operation, for without it there is no real teamwork.

When there is a co-operative atmosphere members are more ready to be involved and committed, and information is shared rather than hidden. Individuals listen to the ideas of others and build on them. People find ways of being more helpful to each other and the team. Co-operation encourages high morale – individuals accept each others' strengths and weaknesses and contribute from their pool of knowledge and skills. All abilities, knowledge and experience are fully utilised by the team and individuals have no inhibitions about using other people's abilities to help with their problems. Problems are shared.

Where true co-operation is alive a degree of conflict is also seen as a necessary and useful part of organisational life. The effective team works through issues of conflict and uses the result to help achieve objectives. Conflict is so often seen as the opposite of co-operation. It is true that if a group of people are in constant disagreement they will find achievement difficult, but a certain amount of conflict also prevents a team becoming complacent and lazy and often is the source of new ideas. Traditionally, conflict has been seen as something caused by trouble makers or 'prima donnas' and something which by definition can be avoided or stifled. A more enlightened approach to conflict suggests that it is inevitable and an integral part of the process of change. If this is true, the management of conflict should be an aid to co-operation, not an obstacle. However, there are two sides to conflict. One is destructive and unhealthy, the other constructive and healthy. Destructive conflict, which defeats co-operation, can occur when individuals' carefully built images are threatened, when personalities intrude, when conflict is expected and the expectation becomes self-fulfilling or when two parties are arguing about different things without realising it. Constructive, healthy conflict has a problem solving base. Those involved in solving the problems are willing to sublimate personality differences, to listen to others' views, to be open and candid to each other, to be supportive and helpful. With such behaviour, not only is each problem solved with total commitment, but subsequent team interaction becomes more effective, and co-operation improves.

Resolving unhelpful conflict means:

(a) examining what is causing trouble between people or groups;

(b) bringing the parties together to discuss the issues involved and to analyse their constituents;

(c) clarifying expectations and roles;

(d) learning how to utilise constructive feedback and value openness;

(e) learning how and when third parties can be helpful;

(f) reaching agreements about future action.

Lecturette 5:
Sound procedures

The effective team thinks results first and methods second but also realises that sound working methods and decision-making lead to achievement of objectives. But, of course, objectives need to be clearly and completely understood by all team members before good decision-making can commence. Clarifying objectives is essential as it can prevent all the misunderstandings and defensive arguments that result from some people not knowing what is happening. In making decisions, good teams develop the ability to collect information quickly and then discuss the alternatives openly. They then become committed to their decisions and ensure that action ensues quickly.

Crucial issues to consider are:

1   How is decision-making accomplished?
(a) Is it mainly formal or informal?
(b) At what levels are decisions taken?
(c) Are people who will be affected really involved?
(d) Is information collected properly and by the proper people?
(e) Do people have the right information?
(f) Is gossip used?
(g) Do power groups operate, and if so are they harmful?
2   How are decisions implemented?
(a) Do those who make decisions give the necessary authority for others to implement them?
(b) Are decisions communicated effectively?
(c) Are the right resources available and present?
(d) Are resources co-ordinated?
(e) Are people resistant to change, and if so how should we overcome this?
3   How are decisions reviewed?
(a) Who carries out the review?

(b) How often is it carried out?
(c) Does review really change things?

Decision-making is one of the basic processes involved in any manager's job, yet it is a process which is so often badly done, for example, at the wrong level in the organisation with incomplete information, or carried out by people remote from the decision and thus not committed to it. To arrive at good decisions a flexible and explicit working procedure must exist which all members understand and adhere to.

The manager or team leader is the key man in determining the degree to which a team will participate in decision-making. There are four decision-making approaches which a leader can use. No leader could use one approach all of the time but the important thing is which of them is the preferred approach and which does he seek to utilise when circumstances allow.

1   *'I make the decisions around here.'* The leader solves the problem without asking the opinions of others or giving them an opportunity to contribute.

2   *'I will seek your opinion before I decide.'* The leader still makes the decision but based on opinions and information which he solicits from team members.

3   *'I take decisions with people of my choice.'* Here the leader takes decisions with certain team members whom he selects.

4   *'We take the decisions.'* Here the leader brings the problem before the team who discuss it and together they take the decision. The team may 'delegate' the decisions to an individual or subgroup if they consider that appropriate.

Perhaps the first question is: 'Are decisions being made in the right place in the organisation?' In other words, are they being made at the right level, are they our decisions or do they belong to someone else? This needs to be considered both in terms of available and accurate information and whether the decision-making process helps to motivate the people who have to carry out the action resulting from it.

Effective decision-making by teams must rest upon a general consensus of agreement that the decision is a good one. It is not, however, merely a compromise since individuals are not afraid to disagree, and are listened to carefully.

Effective teams decide what information is needed, and allocate the collection of this to the most appropriate members. In order to do this roles and relationships must be clearly understood. This information is then openly and frankly discussed. Members are aware of their own values and those of people in the organisation; they recognise the bias and prejudice that these values can have on decisions. They take into account the consequences of alternative decisions for departments, the organisation, individuals, customers and suppliers, etc. When the decision is made there is commitment to it and the team ensures that action follows. Plans are made for implementation, again using the team's knowledge and skills as effectively as possible, and the resultant action is closely watched. People care about the quality of the decisions and are willing to learn from its consequences. They are also willing to modify the implementation if it does not seem to be working out.

To sum up, there are five main stages in effective decision-making:

1   A clear understanding of the reasons for taking a decision, i.e. the problem or opportunity.
2   An analysis of the nature of the problem.
3   An examination of alternative solutions, a weighting of these and a consideration of their likely consequences.
4   The implementation of the decision, including overcoming resistance.
5   A review and evaluation of the decision.

Lecturette 6:
Appropriate leadership

Not all teams need leaders of a permanent nature, and many developed teams are able to change their leadership to suit the circumstances. But whether led or managed continually by the same person or by a variety of people we all have views about the way in which we should be managed. Successful managers the world over differ in what they regard as good management but what all agree on is that the team that is dissatisfied with the way in which it is led will operate below maximum effectiveness. We all know the manager who rules by fear, who gets results by shouting, ordering and threatening. Often he appears to get the results he requires but he is unlikely to lead a team of committed people all giving their best. By contrast there is the weak and ineffectual manager. He may be a nice, friendly sort of guy whom everyone likes on a personal level but too often he lacks the will or ability to face up to the difficult issues which confront him. Observers have noticed repeatedly that the way people lead and manage others is a product of the attitudes and assumptions they have about them. Douglas McGregor developed a model which shows this quite clearly and some of the activities about leadership included earlier are based on the model. It is a simple and effective way of explaining some of the major issues about leadership.

He noticed that one set of managers displayed a set of assumptions about others which he called Theory X. They appeared to believe that people:

(a)   were fundamentally lazy and had to be pushed to work;
(b)   were basically sly and only interested in their own benefit;
(c)   responded best when disciplined and controlled;
(d)   took notice of punishment and worked better because of it;
(e)   were not really interested in their jobs or the welfare of the organisation and only worked against their will.

Another set of managers displayed assumptions which were fundamentally different and which he called Theory Y. These managers appeared to believe that people:

(a) were fundamentally willing to work providing the jobs were meaningful;
(b) were basically honest;
(c) took an active interest in the welfare of the groups to which they belonged;
(d) responded best when given responsibility and freedom of action and manoeuvre;
(e) valued honest praise and resented excessive punishment;
(f) were very interested in the quality of their working lives as well as their personal lives.

He also noticed that those managers exhibiting the Theory Y assumptions consistently obtained better results and that their departments had higher outputs, their people showed more creativity and innovation, they had fewer labour problems and lower labour turnover, they had less waste and were generally able to obtain better and more profitable results.

This all sounds very simple until we look around and see many thousands of managers who appear to practise the Theory X assumptions and yet are very successful. Often this is because their own personal ability can get them the results they desire without needing to get the best out of others. However, good teamwork gets the best out of all the members of the team and that demands management or leadership style which is both flexible and appropriate.

Another key for the leader to get the most out of himself and his team is delegation. Delegation is not only a way of enabling a leader or manager to devote time to other issues, it is also real management development and a key to the confidence a leader really feels for his team. Where delegation does not happen it is a barrier to both increased results for the team and development for the manager and his subordinates. Often a low level of delegation results from lack of confidence in subordinates, lack of time to train and develop subordinates or fear of the results of delegation. There are countless examples of managers not coping because they have too much to do and yet they accuse those who surround them of being 'idle or unenthusiastic'. Delegation should enhance rather than threaten a manager's status and any manager who claims that he is indispensible is usually not delegating as he should. Many managers find that effective delegation is based on the following:

1   A simple analysis of areas of accountability and those which it is possible to delegate.
2   A consideration both of which team members could tackle the area and which would welcome it as a development opportunity.
3   A consideration of the training which would be necessary for delegation to take place.

Chosen team members should always be willing to take on the extra responsibilities and the leader must be prepared to give full authority and support. There are often risks in delegation but although improvement and development often demand risks they also bring high rewards. Finally, always remember to review the progress of the delegation and be prepared to take action if things go wrong.

In observing really successful team leaders, ten characteristics of success frequently stand out. The successful team leader:

(a)   is authentic and true to himself and his own beliefs;
(b)   uses delegation as aid to achievement and development;
(c)   is clear about the standards he wishes to achieve;
(d)   is willing and able to give and receive trust and loyalty;
(e)   has the personal strength to maintain the integrity and position of his team;
(f)   is receptive to people's hopes, needs and dignity;
(g)   faces facts honestly and squarely;
(h)   encourages personal and team development;
(i)   establishes and maintains sound working procedures;
(j)   tries to make work a happy and rewarding place.

Lecturette 7:
Regular review

Good teams understand not only the team's character and its role in the organisation, but they look at the way the team works, how it makes decisions, deals with conflicts, etc.

Reviewing allows the team to learn from experience and to consciously improve teamwork. There are numerous ways of reviewing and all of them are essentially concerned with team members receiving feedback about their performance as individuals or about the performance of the team as a whole. The three most widely used ways of reviewing are described below.

THE TEAM REVIEWING ITS OWN PERFORMANCE

There are many different approaches and aids to doing this and some are contained within this book. The skills which a team needs to carry out meaningful reviews are not easy to acquire because they depend upon the development of some of the other characteristics explained earlier. For instance, both openness and trust are needed in ample quantities if the exercise is to be realistic. These skills and the willingness to use them can be encouraged by stressing the really positive contribution which regular review can make. Review can often be carried out during and after the completion of a task and once the skills have been mastered it becomes a way of life for the team.

USING AN OBSERVER

The most popular method is usually called 'process review' and it involves someone sitting outside the group and quietly observing what happens. Often he will have a prompt sheet which reminds him of the various items to be observed. He is really looking for the acts or words which helped the group in its task and those which did not, and at the end of the task, or at some convenient time during it, he is invited to present his observations to them for discussion. He must, of course, be careful to report only what he saw and not colour the facts with his own opinions. The skills of really good process observations are again difficult to acquire but anyone who has mastered them can be a real help in the development of effective teams and of individuals.

CLOSED CIRCUIT TELEVISION

In the hands of someone who is both a skilled observer and a skilled operator of the equipment CCTV can be a most powerful tool. The team can be recorded when it is performing a task and then the whole or part of the recording is played back. Whenever a team member requests it or whenever the operator thinks it appropriate the tape can be stopped and the team given the opportunity to analyse the incident just shown. All are able to see for themselves what actually happened and individuals are able to observe the effects on the team of their own interventions. In this way learning can be greatly speeded up and although equipment is expensive to purchase or to hire the savings in time and increases in learning usually more than justify its use.

Clearly, a CCTV set cannot be included with this manual nor can detailed guidance on its use be given here, but the 'Activities' section includes a variety of review instruments which can be used by team members or by observers. All of them have been effectively used many times to help teambuilding.

Regular review can improve team performance by:

(a)   ensuring that adequate effort is directed towards planning;
(b)   improving decision-making;
(c)   increasing support, trust, openness and honesty;
(d)   clarifying objectives;
(e)   identifying development needs and opportunities;
(f)   increasing the effectiveness of team leadership;
(g)   making meetings more productive and more enjoyable;
(h)   decreasing the number of emergencies and crises;
(i)   increasing involvement and commitment.

It is simply a question of learning how to function more effectively in the future by looking at the way the team is operating in the present.

Lecturette 8:
Individual development

Effective teamwork seeks to pool the skills of individuals and to produce better results by so doing. Whilst the effectiveness of the team can be greater than the sum of the parts it also follows that effective teams need to pay attention to the development of individual skills. Just as different societies have different views of the developed group so throughout the history of man different societies and cultures have had different views as to what constitutes the developed and effective individual. As one obvious fact about teams is that they are a collection of individuals, then their effectiveness must in part be a function of individual ability.

Often when organisations look at personal development issues they are seen in terms of the skills and knowledge which individuals possess and training strategies are geared to improving them. But, of course, it is never as simple as that. Business life is full of countless examples of executives who seem to have all the right skills and all the knowledge, technical and otherwise, and yet still never seem to achieve worthwhile results. We also meet many executives, particularly owner-managers, who have had little training and on the surface appear deficient in the accepted managerial skills, and yet they have created immensely successful businesses and seem to have the knack of always succeeding. In practice, management is not simply a question of skills and textbook knowledge, it is about seeing opportunities, seizing them and making things happen, and some people seem able to do that continually. Observers have noticed that the most effective and the least effective almost invariably display two different sets of characteristics (see page 204). The less effective seem to have a passive approach to life wishing to be undisturbed as much as possible. They find challenge frightening and avoid it whenever possible. They also avoid insight into themselves and their beliefs. They do not welcome feedback from others and criticism, far from being healthy, is seen as unhelpful and threatening. They are not in touch with their own feelings, and do not wish to be, and new experiences are avoided because of the potential threat which they could bring. Often they try to manipulate others and seldom do they seek to increase the freedom of others. They lack concern for others and whilst they may give sympathy to them they rarely offer real help. Their beliefs are basically the beliefs of others, often learned in childhood and seldom seriously questioned; they are not authentic people. They are intolerant of the views of others and are often heard to bemoan the fact that others are not like them. In their unrelaxed posture towards life they are content with low standards for themselves and for others and when difficult problems arise they are the first to shun responsibility. For them life would be happier if they were surrounded by weak people but they are not and so often they resent the strong who they see contributing substantially to their basically unhappy and unsatisfactory lives.

Successful people by contrast seem to have an active approach to life. They are the people who make things happen and are constantly seeking new challenges for themselves and the groups which they represent. They wish to know more about themselves and are interested in the feedback which others can give them about both their strengths and their weaknesses. They welcome constructive criticism. They recognise that time and energy are limited in terms of human existence and, seeing them as man's most valuable resources, they plan their lives to make the most of them. They constantly seek new experiences because they see the quality of life being linked to the range of experience which an individual can encompass. By constantly achieving good results they build a reputation as people who can be relied upon to 'come up with the goods' and they are committed to seeing things through even when difficult situations arise. They understand their own feelings and try to use them as a positive force in their relationships with others. They care about others and their feelings and whilst they may not always agree they remain tolerant to the beliefs of those around them. They strive to be open with others, for they have nothing to hide and they realise that honesty is a much neglected value but is usually the best course. They are not frightened to give freedom to others, realising that personal growth requires room to grow. They set high standards for themselves and the groups which they represent and are constantly seeking opportunities to extend themselves and their colleagues. Because they have worked things through for themselves they are clear about their own beliefs and are not inhibited by the teachings of others. Because they are successful they are strong and they rejoice in that strength using it as a positive force for themselves and their colleagues. They are relaxed, happy people who see life as an adventure which they enjoy immensely.

Usually, no-one displays totally either one or the other set of characteristics; it is a question of degree, and individual development is essentially about which set of characteristics we move towards and which we move away from. The two sets of characteristics when placed side by side become stark alternatives; choices which we are able to make about ourselves, our approach to life and our approach to work. Often those individuals who predominantly exhibit the high effectiveness characteristics are uncomfortable people to work with, their drive and dynamism at first sight appearing to inhibit the common good of the team. The really effective teams, however, learn to capitalise on these qualities and encourage their less effective members to move towards them.

SUMMARY OF HIGH/LOW EFFECTIVENESS
CHARACTERISTICS

High effectiveness characteristics	*Low effectiveness characteristics*
1 Active	1 Passive
2 Seek challenge	2 Avoid challenge
3 Seek insight into themselves	3 Avoid self-knowledge
4 See and use time and energy as valuable resources	4 Misuse time and energy
5 In touch with their feelings	5 Out of touch with their feelings
6 Show concern for others	6 Do not care for others' feelings
7 Relaxed	7 Tense
8 Open and honest	8 Use manipulation
9 Stretch themselves	9 Avoid stretching experiences
10 Clear personal values	10 Programmed by the views of others
11 Set high standards	11 Set low standards
12 Welcome feedback	12 Avoid feedback
13 See things through	13 Opt out
14 Tolerate and use opposing views	14 Intolerant to others' views
15 Use conflict constructively	15 Avoid conflict
16 Give freedom	16 Restrain freedom
17 Are happy about life	17 Unhappy about life

Lecturette 9:
Sound inter-group relations

No man is an island and rarely is a team. No matter how well a team exhibits

(a) clear objectives,
(b) openness and confrontation,
(c) support and trust,
(d) co-operation and conflict,
(e) sound procedures,
(f) appropriate leadership,
(g) regular review,
(h) individual development,

its success will be hindered if it lacks good relationships with other groups or individuals. The cohesive team can so often appear as a threat to other groups who perceive that they are less effective and this can so easily lead to cool relationships or hostility. Just as teamwork is individuals working well together so effective organisational life is partially teams relating to and performing well together. Thus, the really effective team is constantly reaching out to others to ensure that its efforts are well received and supported and to ensure that help from others will be forthcoming when needed.

Effective external relationships are:

1   Ensuring that the actions and decisions of the team are communicated and understood.
2   Recognising that although teams are not the same that is no reason for them to stay apart.
3   Trying to understand the other team's point of view, recognising their problems and difficulties and offering a hand of friendship when needed.

4   Continually seeking out ways of working effectively with others.
5   Not being too rigid in defending team boundaries.
6   Recognising that boundaries and responsibilities between teams will need to be reviewed and amended from time to time.
7   Anticipating and eliminating potential inter-team problems before they arise.
8   Really trying to listen to others and doing all that is possible to help them listen to you.
9   Using others as a source of ideas and comparison.
10 Understanding and utilising differences in people.

Once achieved, effective inter-group relationships bring a host of advantages. Amongst the foremost of these are greater ability to influence the organisation, more available help, easier flow of information, easier problem solving, less anxiety and happier, more enjoyable working lives.

It follows that to have sound external relationships teams must exhibit and use many of the characteristics outlined earlier. Many of the building blocks of effective teamwork are also the bridges to other teams. Many teams have foundered because, although they were highly developed internally, they omitted to build those bridges which are so necessary to link the team with other parts of the organisation.

PART III

FURTHER INFORMATION

The theory and activities which have been included so far have been chosen both for their effectiveness and because they are relatively easy to understand and apply without expert help. It is hoped that most users will find their needs met by this selection.

In this section are sources of further ideas and assistance which will be of use to those who have not found the answer to their particular teambuilding needs within this book or wish to study the subject in greater depth. They are listed under the headings: 1 Reading list, 2 Films and tapes, 3 Consultants, 4 Other useful organisations. I have included principally items which I know other managers have found useful but clearly you will need to make your own choice as to suitability.

1
Reading list

Adair, J., Ayres R., Debenham, I.Y., Després D (eds.) *A Handbook of Management Training Exercises,* British Association for Industrial & Commercial Education, London, 1978.

Argyle, M., *Social Interaction*, Methuen, London, 1969.

Argyris, C., *Intervention Theory and Method: A Behavioural Science View*, Addison-Wesley, London, 1970.

Beveridge, W.E., *The Interview in Staff Appraisal*, Allen & Unwin, London, 1975.

Bradford, L.P., *Making Meetings Work*, University Associates, La Jolla, California, 1976.

Buzan, T., *Use Your Head*, BBC Publications, London, 1975.

Chilver, J.W., *Human Aspects of Management: A Case Study Approach*, Pergamon, Oxford, 1976.

Clarron, C.G., Eves, S.M. and Fenner, E.C., *Behaviour: A Guide for Managers*, Macmillan, London, 1976.

Cohen, A.M. and Smith, R.D., *The Critical Incident in Growth Groups*, University Associates, La Jolla, California, 1976.

Crosby, R.P., *Planning Recommendations or Actions: A Team Development Guidebook*, University Associates, La Jolla, California, 1972.

Dyar, D.A. and Giles, W.J., *Improving Skills in Working With People: Interaction Analysis*, HMSO, London, 1974.

Dyer, W.F., *Teambuilding Issues and Alternatives*, Addison-Wesley, Massachusetts and London, 1977.

Eddy, W.B. *et al.*, *Behavioural Science and The Manager's Role*, University Associates, La Jolla, California, 1976.

Ends, E.J. and Page, C.W., *Organisational Teambuilding*, Winthrop, Cambridge, Massachusetts, 1977.

Food, Drink and Tobacco Industry Training Board, *Development at Work*, Food, Drink and Tobacco Industry Training Board, Gloucester, 1978.

Ford, G.A. and Lippitt, G.L., *Planning Your Future: A Workbook for Personal Goal-setting*, University Associates, La Jolla, California, 1976.

Fordyce, J.K. and Weil, R., *Managing With People*, Addison-Wesley, London, 1971.

Francis, D. and Woodcock, M., *People At Work: A Practical Guide to Organisational Change*, University Associates, La Jolla, California, 1975.

Hague, H., *Executive Self-development: Real Learning in Real Situations*, Macmillan, London, 1974.

Harris, T.A., *I'm OK, You're OK*, Pan Books, London, 1973.

Harrison, R., 'Role negotiations', in *Readings in Organisational Psychology*, Prentice-Hall, London, 1974.

Honey, P., *Face To Face: A Practical Guide to Interactive Skills*, Institute of Personnel Management, 1976.

Humble, J. (ed.), *Improving The Performance of The Experienced Manager*, McGraw-Hill, Maidenhead, 1973.

James, M. and Jongeward, D., *Born to Win*, Addison-Wesley, London, 1973.

Jones, J.E. and Pfeiffer, J.W., *Handbooks of Structured Experiences*, vols. 1, 2, 3, 4, 5, 6, University Associates, La Jolla, California.

Kepner, C.H. and Tregoe, B.B., *The Rational Manager: Systematic Approach to Problem Solving and Decision Making*, McGraw-Hill, Maidenhead, 1965.

Kirn, A.G. and Kirn, M., *Lifework Planning*, McGraw-Hill, New York, 1978.

Lawrence, P.R. and Lorsch, J.W., *Developing Organisations: Diagnosis and Action*, Addison-Wesley, London, 1969.

Lievegoed, B.C.J., *The Developing Organisation*, Tavistock, London, 1973.

Lippitt, G.L., *Visualising Change*, University Associates, La Jolla, California, 1976.

Lippitt, G.L., This, L.E. and Bidwell, R.G., *Optimising Human Resources: Readings in Individual and Organisational Development*, Addison-Wesley, London 1971.

McGregor, D., *The Human Side of Enterprise*, McGraw-Hill, Maidenhead, 1960.

Maier, N.F., *The Appraisal Interview: Three Basic Approaches*, University Associates, La Jolla, California, 1976.

Margerison, C.J., *Managing Effective Work Groups*, McGraw-Hill, Maidenhead, 1973.

Merry, U. and Allerhand, M., *Developing Teams and Organisations*, Addison-Wesley, London, 1977.

Morris, J. and Burgoyne, J., *Developing Resourceful Managers*, Institute of Personnel Management, London, 1973.

Perls, F.S., *In and Out the Garbage Pail*, Bantam Books, London, 1972, Real People Press, Utah, 1969.

Pfeiffer, J.W. and Jones, J.E., *Annual Handbooks for Group Facilitators 1972, 1973, 1974, 1975, 1976, 1977, 1978*, University Associates, La Jolla, California.

Pfeiffer, J.W. and Heslin, R., *Instrumentation in Human Relations Training*, University Associates, La Jolla, California, 1972.

Rackham, N. and Morgan, T., *Behaviour Analysis in Training*, McGraw-Hill, Maidenhead, 1977.

Rackham, N., Honey, P. and Colbert, M., *Developing Interactive Skills*, Wellens Publishing, Guilsborough, 1971.

Randell, G.A. *et al.*, *Staff Appraisal*, Institute of Personnel Management, London, 1974.

Reddin, W.J., *Effective Management by Objectives*, Management Publications Ltd, London, 1971.

Revans, R.W., *Developing Effective Managers: A New Approach to Business Education*, Longman, Harlow, 1971.

Roberts, T., *Developing Effective Managers*, Institute of Personnel Management, London, 1974.

Schein, E., *Process Consultation*, Addison-Wesley, London, 1969.

Schein, E., *Organisational Psychology*, Prentice-Hall, London, 1970.

Schindler-Rainman, E., Lippitt, R. and Cole, J., *Taking Your Meetings Out of the Doldrums*, University Associates, La Jolla, California, 1977.

Schollick, N. and Bloxsom, P., *Staff Appraisal – Self Appraisal: a Programme Guide to Staff Appraisal Interviews*, Godwin, London, 1975.

Scott, B. and Edwards, B., *Appraisal and Appraisal Interviewing*, Industrial Society, London, 1973.

Sidney, E., Brown, M. and Argyle, M., *Skills With People: A Guide For Managers*, Hutchinson, London, 1973.

Singer, E.J., *Effective Management Coaching*, Institute of Personnel Management, London, 1974.

Smith, P.B., *Improving Skills in Working With People: The T-group*, HMSO, London, 1969.

Sperry, L. and Hess, L.R., *Contact Counselling: Communication Skills for People in Organisations*, Addison-Wesley, London, 1974.

Torrington, D.P. and Sutton, D.F. (eds.), *Handbook of Management Development*, Gower Press, London, 1973.

Williams, M.R., *Performance Appraisal in Management*, Heinemann, London, 1972.

2
Films and tapes

Appraising performance: an interview skills course
Norman R.F. Maier
(2 cassette sound tapes and facilitator's guide)
University Associates, 1976.

Coaching for results
Training Services Agency (now Training Services Division of the
   Manpower Services Commission)
(2 × 16 mm colour films and trainer's guide)
Millbank Films, 1976.

Employee and team development
Betty Beizon and Lawrence N. Solomon
(4 cassette sound tapes and facilitator's guide)
University Associates, 1976.

Successful staff appraisal
Management Training Limited
(16 mm film and sound tape and leader's guide)
Guild Sound and Union Limited, 1971.

Team building and *Confronting conflict*
Sheldon A. Davis
(2 × 16 mm films and leader's guides)
Guild Sound and Vision Limited.

Where do you go from here?
Rank Aldis
(16 mm film)
Rank Audio Visual Limited, 1975.

3
Consultants

Coverdale Training Ltd
270 Earls Court Road
London SW5 9AS

Dale Loveluck Associates
Little Oaks
Mitchell Walk
Amersham
Buckinghamshire

EMAS
Southover House
Rusper Road
Ilfield
Crawley
West Sussex RH11 0LN

Industrial Training Service
73/75 Mortimer Street
London W1N 8HY

People at Work (Resources Limited)
Mount Ararat Road
Richmond
Surrey

The Anne Shaw Organisation Ltd
Brook Lane
Alderley Edge
Cheshire SK9 7QH

In addition the following two organisations have members who are well qualified to help with organisation teambuilding.

Group Relations Training Association
56 Milbank Road
Darlington
Co Durham DL3 9NH

Organisation Development
 Network
ODN Secretariat
Hatchetts
Bytchers Lane
Preston
Hitchin
Hertfordshire SG4 7TR

4
Other useful organisations

These are listed because they have publications, undertake assignments, give advice, run courses or supply information on human relations/teambuilding topics.

BACIE
16 Part Crescent
Regent's Park
London W1N 4AP

British Institute of Management
Management House
Parker Street
London WC2B 5PT

Confederation of British Industry
Tothill Street
London SW1H 9LP

Department of Employment
St James's Square
London SW1Y 4JB

Guardian Business Services
21 St John Street
London WC1

Industrial Society
48 Bryanston Square
London W1H 8AH
and
Peter Runge House
3 Carlton House Terrace
London SW1Y 5DG

Institute of Personnel Management
Central House
Upper Woburn Place
London WC1H 0HX

Manpower Services Commission
Selkirk House
166 High Holborn
London WC1V 6PF

National Economic Development
  Office
Millbank Tower
Millbank
London SW1P 4QX

Trades Union Congress
Congress House
Great Russell Street
London WC1B 3LS

Training Services Division
(Manpower Services Commission)
162-168 Regent Street
London W1R 6DE

Workers' Educational Association
9 Upper Berkeley Street
London W1

COLLEGES AND MANAGEMENT CENTRES

Anglian Regional Management Centre
Danbury Park
Danbury
Chelmsford CM3 4AT

Ashridge Management College
(Industrial Relations Resource
    Centre)
Berkhamsted
Hertfordshire HP4 1NS

Bristol Polytechnic
Coldharbour Lane
Bristol BS16 1QY

City University Graduate Business
    Centre
Gresham College
Basinghall Street
London EC2V 5AH

Cranfield School of Management
Cranfield
Bedford MK43 0AL

Derby College of Art and
    Technology
Kedleston Road
Derby DE3 1GB

Glasgow College of Technology
North Hanover Place
Glasgow G4 0BA

Kingston Polytechnic
Penrhn Road
Kingston-upon-Thames
KT1 2EE

Leicester Polytechnic
P.O. Box 143
Leicester LE1 9BH

Liverpool Polytechnic
Richmond House
1 Rumford Place
Liverpool L3 9RH

London Business School
Sussex Place
Regents Park
London NW1 4SA

Manchester Business School
University of Manchester
Booth Street West
Manchester M15 6PB

Mid-Essex Technical College
    and School of Art
Victoria Road South
Chelmsford CM1 1LL

North East London Polytechnic
Romford Road
London E15 4LZ

North Staffordshire Polytechnic
College Road
Stoke-on-Trent ST4 2DE

Oxford Polytechnic
Headington
Oxford OX3 0BP

Paisley College of Technology
Colinton Road
Edinburgh EH10 5DT

Polytechnic of Wales
Treforest
Pontypridd
Wales CF37 1CL

Portsmouth Polytechnic
Museum Road
Portsmouth PO1 2QQ

Roffey Park Management College
Horsham
Sussex RH12 4TD

Scottish Business School
69 St George's Place
Glasgow G2 1EU

Sheffield Polytechnic
Grove Road
Totley Rise
Sheffield
Yorkshire S17 4DJ

Sunderland Polytechnic
Chester Road
Sunderland SR1 3SD

Teeside Polytechnic
Borough Road
Middlesbrough
Cleveland TS1 3BA

Thames Regional Management Centre
Slough College of Higher Education
Wellington Street
Slough SL1 11G

The Polytechnic of Central
London
309 Regent Street
London W1R 8AL

The Polytechnic of Wolverhampton
Wulfruna Street
Wolverhampton WV1 1LY

The St Helens College of
Technology
St Helens WA10 1PZ

Trent Polytechnic
Burton Street
Nottingham NG1 4BU

University of Aston
158 Corporation Street
Birmingham B4 6TE

University of Bath School of
Management
Claverton Down
Bath BA2 7AY

University of Lancaster
School of Management and
Organisational Sciences
Fillow House
Lancaster LA1 4YX

University of Sheffield
Division of Economic Studies
Sheffield S10 2TN

INDUSTRIAL TRAINING BOARDS

Industrial Training Boards cover the vast majority of industries in the UK. They are Government sponsored but each one is controlled by a tripartite structure of employer, trade union and educational representatives, and all offer an advisory service to firms within the industries which they cover. Some have done valuable work in the area of teambuilding and can offer relevant publications, training events and advice but discretion needs to be exercised by the user.

In particular, it is worth bearing in mind that:

1 Boards do not all have the same views about development needs in their industries.

2 Some Boards have done little work in the team development area and do not have real expertise to offer.

3 The skill and experience of the adviser is all-important so do not be afraid to challenge and question his views and the advice he gives. If he is worth his salt he will respect you for it, if he does not then you are probably better off without his advice.

Some boards also offer an information service and will lend out useful publications.

The following is a complete list of Industrial Training Boards:

Agricultural ITB
Bourne House
32/34 Beckenham Road
Beckenham
Kent BR3 4PB

Air Transport and Travel ITB
Staines House
158/162 High Street
Staines
Middlesex TW18 4AS

Carpet ITB
Evelyn House
32 Alderley Road
Wilmslow
Cheshire SK9 1NX

Ceramics, Glass and Mineral
        Products ITB
Bovis House
Northolt Road
Harrow
Middlesex HA2 0FF

Chemical and Allied Products ITB
Staines House
158 High Street
Middlesex TW18 4AT

Clothing and Allied Products ITB
10th Floor
Tower House
Merrion Way
Leeds LS2 8NY

Construction ITB
Radnor House
1272 London Road
Norbury
London SW16 4EL

Cotton and Allied Textiles ITB
10th Floor
Sunlight House
Quay Street
Manchester M3 3LH

Distributive ITB
Maclaren House
Talbot Road
Stretford
Manchester M32 0FP

Engineering ITB
54 Clarendon Road
Watford WD1 1LB

Food, Drink and Tobacco ITB
Barton House
Barton Street
Gloucester GL1 1QQ

Footwear, Leather and Fur
    Skin ITB
Maney Building
29 Birmingham Road
Sutton Coldfield
West Midlands B72 1QE

Foundry ITC
50/54 Charlotte Street
London W1P 2EL

Furniture and Timber ITB
31 Octagon Parade
High Wycombe
Buckinghamshire HP11 2JA

Hotel and Catering ITB
Ramsey House
Central Square
Wembley HA9 7AP

Iron and Steel ITB
4 Little Essex Street
London WC2R 3LH

Knitting, Lace and Net ITB
4 Hamilton Road
Nottingham NG5 1AU

Local Government ITB
8 The Arndale Centre
Luton LU1 2TS

Man Made Fibres Producing ITB
Langwood House
63-81 High Street
Rickmansworth
Hertfordshire WD3 1EQ

Paper and Paper Products ITB
Star House
Potters Bar
Hertfordshire EN6 2PG

Petroleum ITB
York House
Empire Way
Wembley
Middlesex HA9 0PT

Printing and Publishing ITB
Merit House
Edgware Road
London NW9 5AG

Road Transport ITB
Capitol House
Empire Way
Wembley HA9 0NG

Rubber and Plastics Processing ITB
Brent House
950 Great West Road
Brentford
Middlesex TW8 9ES

Shipbuilding ITB
Raeburn House
Northolt Road
South Harrow
Middlesex HA2 0DR

National Water Council
   (Training Division)
Tadley Court
Tadley Common Road
Tadley
Nr Basingstoke
Hampshire RG26 6TB

Wool Jute and Flax ITB
Butterfield House
Otley Road
Basildon
Shipley
West Yorkshire BD17 7HE